# Hungary

## Poverty and Social Transfers

The World Bank
Washington, D.C.

Copyright © 1996
The International Bank for Reconstruction
and Development/ THE WORLD BANK
1818 H Street, N.W.
Washington, D.C. 20433, U.S.A.

World Bank Country Studies are among the many reports originally prepared for internal use as part of the continuing analysis by the Bank of the economic and related conditions of its developing member countries and of its dialogues with the governments. Some of the reports are published in this series with the least possible delay for the use of governments and the academic, business and financial, and development communities. The typescript of this paper therefore has not been prepared in accordance with the procedures appropriate to formal printed texts, and the World Bank accepts no responsibility for errors. Some sources cited in this paper may be informal documents that are not readily available.

The World Bank does not guarantee the accuracy of the data included in this publication and accepts no responsibility whatsoever for any consequence of their use. The boundaries, colors, denominations, and other information shown on any map in this volume do not imply on the part of the World Bank Group any judgment on the legal status of any territory or the endorsement or acceptance of such boundaries.

The complete backlist of publications from the World Bank is shown in the annual *Index of Publications*, which contains an alphabetical title list (with full ordering information) and indexes of subjects, authors, and countries and regions. The latest edition is available free of charge from the Distribution Unit, Office of the Publisher, The World Bank, 1818 H Street, N.W., Washington, D.C. 20433, U.S.A., or from Publications, The World Bank, 66, avenue d'Iéna, 75116 Paris, France.

ISSN: 0-0253-2123

**Library of Congress Cataloging-in-Publication Data**

Hungary : poverty and social transfers.
      p.   cm. — (A World Bank country study)
    Includes bibliographical references.
    ISBN 0-8213-3634-7
    1. Poverty—Hungary.   2. Hungary—Economic conditions—1989–
3. Income distribution—Hungary.   4. Transfer payments—Hungary.
I. World Bank.   II. Series.
HC300.295.P6H86   1996
339-4'6'09439— dc20

                               96-15748
                                CIP

# Contents

## TABLES

1.1    The incidence of Poverty and the Poverty Gap: 1989 and 1993
1.2    The Incidence of Poverty in 1993
1.3    Movement of Individuals Between Income Deciles, 1993-94
1.4    Key Economic Indicators 1989-94
1.5    Trends in Household Income from Labor and Cash Transfers: 1989-93
1.6    Income-Earning Status of Household Head and Unemployment
1.7    Poverty Incidence and Poverty Gap by Unemployment Characteristics
1.8    Incidence of Poverty and Poverty Gap by Region
1.9    The Incidence of Poverty and the Poverty Gap by Household Composition and Gender of Household Head
1.10    The Incidence of Poverty and the Poverty Gap by Education of the Household Head
1.11    The Incidence of Poverty and the Poverty Gap by Age of Household Head
1.12    Key Determinants of Poverty

2.1    Major Cash Transfer Programs, 1993: The Numbers
2.2    Distribution of Cash Transfers by Socioeconomic Characteristics
2.3    Distribution of Cash Transfers by Poverty Level
2.4    Poor to NonPoor Cash Transfer Ratios (Shares Captured by Households Below the Minimum Pension)
2.5    Monthly Transfers to One Pretransfer Poor Person - (Average HUF)
2.6    Number of Pretransfer Poor Persons Helped per HUF 1 Million of Transfers
2.7    The Impact of Social Transfers on Alleviating Poverty
2.8    Social Transfers and the Poverty Gap
2.9    Selected Cash Transfer Reforms: Effects on the Incidence of Poverty and Fiscal Viability

## BOXES

## FIGURES

# ACKNOWLEDGEMENTS

This report was written by Christine Allison (task manager) and Christiaan Grootaert (poverty specialist). It draws upon background work done by Peter Szivos (poverty profile), Istvan Toth et. al. (panel data), and Zoltan Fabian (bibliography). Gi-Taik Oh provided research assistance and prepared the graphics. The report was edited by Thomas Good. Laila Tushan, Damika Somasundaram and Zita Debreczeni produced the report. The peer reviewers were Branko Milanovic and Dominique Van De Walle. Michel Noel is the managing Division Chief, and Kemal Dervis the Director.

## Currency Unit
## Hungary Forint (HUF)

### Average Exchange Rates (HUF per US$)

| 1989 | 1990 | 1991 | 1992 | 1993 | 1994 | 1995 |
|---|---|---|---|---|---|---|
| 59.10 | 63.20 | 74.75 | 79.00 | 92.00 | 105.13 | 126.20 |

### List of Acronyms and Abbreviations

| | |
|---|---|
| CPI | Consumer Price Index |
| CSO | Central Statistical Office |
| GDP | Gross Domestic Product |
| GYED | Child Care Fee |
| GYES | Child Care Allowance |
| GYET | Third Child Allowance |
| HBS | Household Budget Survey |
| HIF | Health Insurance Fund |
| HPS | Household Panel Survey |
| HUF | Hungarian Forint |
| OECD | Organisation for Economic Co-operation and Development |
| OLS | Ordinary Least Square |
| TARKI | Social Research Informatics Center |
| THGY | Pregnancy Confinement Allowance |

### Fiscal Year
### January 1 - December 31

# EXECUTIVE SUMMARY

## Introduction

Hungary's transition from a command economy to a market economy has involved important structural changes in the past few years. Although now recording modest GDP growth, the Hungarian economy experienced a four-year long recession (1989-1993) during which almost one fifth of GDP was lost. These forces have inevitably impacted on the welfare of individuals and their families. Primarily through changes in the labor market -- loss of jobs in the state sector, new employment opportunities in the private sector, the emergence of high unemployment and withdrawal from the labor market, deregulation of wages and growing wage dispersion -- disposable household incomes have declined in the aggregate, and the distribution of market incomes has become more unequal. Yet Hungary, like other countries in Central Europe, inherited an extensive system of cash and in-kind benefit programs that was designed to complement low wages and redistribute large amounts of national income. While this system has cushioned the impact of the transition on households in general, the uniform nature of social transfers has led to their failure in preventing increased poverty among those most negatively affected by the economic changes. Social transfers also impose an enormous burden on public expenditures and the economy, and thwart economic growth. Further, cash transfers have an important impact on household and individual behavior through their incentive effects on labor market activity.

How can social transfers be restructured so as to improve their contribution to poverty alleviation, both directly and indirectly, while reducing their impact on the Government budget? This Report attempts to provide some elements of response to this critical question. In doing so, it analyzes the macroeconomic and poverty trends during the period 1989-93, and presents a detailed poverty profile of the population in 1993. Against this background, the report looks at the role of cash social transfers in poverty prevention and poverty alleviation. The report examines the poverty implications of recently agreed changes to cash transfers, and proposes some alternative policy reforms with the objective to improve their contribution to poverty alleviation while reducing their impact on the budget. The report also stresses the importance of achieving poverty reduction through economic growth and associated labor market income gains (new jobs and higher wages). Here too, reducing aggregate expenditure on social transfers, and adjusting elements of transfer programs to encourage pursuit of higher earned incomes (incentive effects) is of equal importance.

## Poverty Trends and Poverty Profile

In the years 1989-93, the *incidence of poverty* (that is, the proportion of the population who falls below a specified household income or expenditure level that defines a "poverty line") increased. For the most part poverty has remained shallow (i.e. incomes or expenditures have fallen only a small distance from the poverty line), but some deep pockets of poverty have developed.

*The Incidence of Poverty Has Increased.* The magnitude of the increase in the incidence of poverty in Hungary is sensitive to the poverty line chosen, the use of income or expenditure data, and to assumptions about income underreporting in household surveys (both recorded and unrecorded in national accounts). Taking the minimum pension as the lowest poverty line, and using unadjusted estimates of income from the 1989 and 1993 Household Budget Surveys, poverty incidence has increased from less than 2 percent of the population in 1989 to over 8 percent in 1993. A poverty line set at approximately one and half times the value of the minimum pension shows that between a third and two fifths of the population was in poverty in 1993 compared to less than 5 percent in 1989.

Two forces lead to greater poverty: a decline in the overall income level, and growing inequality in income distribution. Both trends can be documented for Hungary. The increase in the incidence of poverty is a function primarily of declining real household incomes. And because household incomes are densely concentrated within a small income range (a function of the past when incomes were intentionally compressed), even a small decline in income levels can lead to substantial increases in the incidence of poverty. It is estimated that a variation in monthly income of HUF 500 (US$4) increases the poverty headcount by 3.5 percentage points. A growing income inequality, which in reality is the product of an unequal distribution of the decline in national income, has also played a part in the rising incidence of poverty. The income decline has been most severe for the poorest 5 percent of the population, whose real household expenditure fell by more than a third during the period 1989-93; conversely, the wealthiest income group has actually gained in real terms.

***Poverty is Concentrated Close to the Poverty Line.*** Poverty in Hungary is largely "shallow". That is, the average income (or expenditure) of those below the poverty line is not substantially less than the poverty line, nor substantially less than those just above the poverty line. The *poverty gap*—the average shortfall of household income (expenditure) as a percentage of the poverty line—ranged from 15 to 20 percent from the late 1980s to 1993. But, importantly, the increase in the incidence of poverty has not been associated with any increase in the poverty gap; if anything, the poverty gap has narrowed slightly. This trend is not surprising, as more people whose incomes are close to the poverty line fall just below the line.

***Some Deep Pockets of Poverty Exist.*** As the transition progresses, a new phenomenon is emerging. Within Hungary, there are some households (individuals) whose income falls far short of even the lowest poverty line (the minimum pension). These people number around 500,000 (5 percent of the population) and they should be considered the very poor. Four groups stand out: households headed by a person who has been unemployed for more than a year (*the long-term unemployed*) -- these are typically poorly educated, low skilled, middle-age men; those people with irregular connection to the labor market (*casual employment*), and irregular income; women on extended leave from their jobs to care for young children; and very elderly female pensioners living alone. These people, and their families are bearing the brunt of Hungary's economic transition to a market economy, and they should become the focus of public policy.

***Who Are the Poor in Hungary?*** The groups mentioned above are the very poorest, but others are also vulnerable to poverty. An examination of the characteristics of poverty groups in Hungary yields the following profile:

* Poverty among *pensioners* is slightly above average, but with the exception of elderly females their poverty is shallow.

* In households affected by unemployment, poverty is deeper if the *head of household is unemployed* than if another member of the household is unemployed. *If the head is unemployed and does not receive unemployment insurance benefits,* then incidence of poverty is very high: more than 40 percent of such households have incomes below the minimum pension.

* The regional variation in the incidence of poverty is not very pronounced. Budapest has the

lowest incidence of poverty, while the north/northeast and the south have the highest incidence. Poverty is more pervasive in villages than in cities, most likely reflecting the different labor markets. Indeed, *regional differences in incidence of poverty can be explained entirely by differences in the socioeconomic and demographic composition of the population.*

- Demographic characteristics are important indicators of poverty. The incidence of poverty is lowest in nuclear households with one or two children. It rises steadily with the number of children and is *especially deep in households with two adults and four and more children, and in households with 3 adults and 3 and more children.* Among these households, one in five lives below the minimum pension, and 70 percent are below two-thirds of mean expenditure. The corollary to these findings is that poverty among children is somewhat more pervasive than among the population at large.

- *Poor children live primarily in villages, and in households whose head is poorly educated and does not have more than a temporary attachment to the labor market.* This finding is worrisome since it indicates the likelihood of inter-generational poverty.

- Hungary displays the normal inverse U-shaped lifecycle pattern of poverty, but *the age effect is stronger among the young than the old*, reflecting the relative well-being of pensioners and the high unemployment rate among the young.

- There is a distinct gender dimension to poverty. *Poverty is deeper among female-headed households*, especially if they are single adults with children.

- A strong inverse relationship exists between poverty and the education of the household head. Secondary or higher education virtually guarantees a level of living above the minimum pension, and college and university puts all but 5 percent of the population above the higher poverty line of two-thirds of mean expenditure. Employment, wages and education are all closely correlated.

- When all variables are taken together, *education and labor market status* are found to be the key determinants of poverty, especially for falling below the minimum pension poverty line. Because the Roma (gypsy) population has poor educational attainment and a marginal association with the labor market, the incidence of poverty among this ethnic group is much higher than average.

***Shifts between Transient and Permanent Poverty.*** Some of the population groups in poverty in 1993 were already experiencing poverty prior to the transition. Through the 1980s, poverty was already affecting poorly educated and low-skilled individuals who had limited labor market opportunities as well as large families, the very elderly, and the gypsies. The recession and the structural changes associated with the economic transition have exacerbated their financial situation. New groups have also been lowered into poverty—the unemployed (especially the long-term unemployed who have exhausted their unemployment insurance benefits), mothers (particularly single mothers) on extended child care leave, and persons earning a living from casual employment. The extent to which any of these groups is likely to remain in poverty in the longer run is unclear. There appears to be a great deal of movement by households in and out of various relative income/expenditure positions. Between 1993 and 1994, almost 40 percent of households changed their relative position by two or more deciles. But the change in absolute income (expenditure) of any one household was not great. By contrast, those in the lowest income decile—the poorest—have moved far less, and their characteristics are rather predictable: poor education, young or very old, unemployed over the long-term, and members of the Roma ethnic group.

*Poverty and the Labor Market.* What has determined the winners and losers from the transition thus far? The most important determinant is labor-market status. Income from employment, self-employment, and business (but primarily wage income) is the main contributor to individual and household income. Of sources of household income, employment income (wages) was already the most unequal, and its dispersion across the income groups increased markedly in the transition years. Earnings inequality in Hungary is now on par with that of Western Europe. Labor income is a function of a job-holding, age, education and work skills, and location. Aggregate labor incomes declined by almost as much as the decline in GDP during 1989-93, but the decline was much more a function of job losses than of real wage declines. As such, those who kept a regular job fared reasonably well, particularly in so far as formal-sector jobs provide access to second jobs, an additional source of income. Highly educated employees in private sector companies, often associated with foreign investment, have seen substantial real wage gains. In contrast, less educated and semi-skilled workers and public-sector employees have experienced real wage declines. But the real losers of the transition are the unemployed, casual workers, those on extended child care on state support, and those who have withdrawn from the labor force altogether (in many cases on disability pension arrangements). Their access to regular wage income has essentially ceased.

## The Cash Transfer System

Hungary offers a generous array of cash transfer programs. The transfer system includes contributions-based social insurance, income supplement entitlements, and means-tested social assistance. This report finds that cash transfers are widely distributed in Hungary, benefitting no less than 7 million individuals and 91 percent of households. Of the six transfers examined, pensions, family allowance and social assistance are found to benefit the largest number of households. Pensions alone reach 52 percent of households, and the family allowance reaches 44 percent of households. One of the most striking findings is that the aggregate value of cash transfers is very uniform across households. (While this is not an unexpected outcome for some programs, such as pensions and family allowance, because of the design of those programs, such a flat distribution should not occur with means-tested programs like social assistance.)

*Cash Transfers Have Helped Maintain Disposable Income.* As the share of labor income in aggregate disposable household income has declined in the transition years, cash social transfers which, in the aggregate, maintained their real value through 1993 have become even more important. In 1993, they provided around 38 percent of gross household income, accounting for 20 percent of GDP. In the past two years, public expenditure on cash transfers has fallen, and since the number of recipients has remained largely unchanged, benefit amounts have declined. Different cash transfers have played different roles during the transition—some have been more effective than others at preventing poverty. In general, social insurance-based transfers tied to previous wages and designed to replace wage income (pensions, unemployment insurance benefits and the child care fee) have been most effective at maintaining incomes, largely due to program size and the high value of payments. (These transfers alone account for 15 percent of GDP). Social assistance has been less effective at alleviating poverty, due primarily to poor targeting and inadequate transfer amounts for those most in need.

*But Cash Transfers Fail to Prevent Poverty.* In a static sense, cash transfers have prevented many households from falling into poverty. Indeed, cash transfers have held about 60 percent of households above two-thirds of mean household expenditure, or 45 percent if pensions are excluded. On the other hand, because of their wide distribution and their relative "blindness" to need (or household income level), cash transfers leave many household—including transfer recipient households—in poverty. More than one-quarter of households who receive social transfers remain below the poverty line.

*Cash Transfers Could do Much More to Help the Poor.* Of considerable interest, both as a counterfactual to the recent past and to the present time when expenditure reduction is needed for macroeconomic stabilization reasons, is the extent to which cash transfers could be more effective poverty alleviation tools. (It is acknowledged that they have other important objectives.) It is clear that they could do a great deal more to help the poor. There are two fundamental aspects that prevent more effective poverty alleviation:

- There are too many beneficiaries, but there are also unintentional exclusions, mainly from discretionary (social assistance) programs. Programs would do well to be more narrowly focussed (targeted).

- Because of the large number of beneficiaries and the flatness in their distribution (with respect to household income), cash transfers are of an inadequate amount when they are most needed. Benefits remain largely unreconstructed from the past when there was little income differentiation and uniform payments made sense. That is no longer the case, and the level of benefits needs to be much more carefully tied to need.

The analysis in Chapter 2 demonstrates that there exists a ready capacity to alleviate poverty up to a modest income threshold by redirecting cash transfers -- even excluding pensions -- from the richer groups to the poorer ones. This could be done in different ways for different target groups: compressing public pension benefits and raising the minimum pension for poor pensioners, directing larger family allowance payments at poor families, and reforming the social assistance system. These themes are taken up below.

## Restructuring Social Transfers

There are two aspects to poverty in Hungary: the quite widespread shallow poverty, in one sense, a *relative* poverty phenomenon, and the small but deep pockets of poverty. (Shallow poverty comprises people close to the higher poverty line; deep poverty comprises those who fall below the minimum pension poverty line.) These patterns of poverty are not dissimilar from those in Western Europe and other Western countries.

Yet income distribution in Hungary is still much more equal than in neighboring Western countries, and the respective roles of market incomes and social incomes are still quite different. In Hungary, market - or earned - incomes constitute a much smaller share of total disposable household income than in most western economies. Addressing poverty starts by redressing this imbalance: at the aggregate, market incomes must rise, and social incomes must fall. The two are not unconnected. (See the recent Country Economic Memorandum[1].)

*Dealing with Shallow Poverty.* The appropriate policy response to the phenomenon of shallow poverty is complicated, not least of which because people in this poverty category are a heterogeneous

---

[1]    Hungary: Structural Reforms for Sustainable Growth. A World Bank Country Study, 1995.

group; included here are some pensioners, low-paid employees, some of the unemployed, and some of the households with a large number of children. The appropriate policy responses for each of these groups differ. Moreover, evidence suggests that the movement of people (households) in and out of shallow poverty is substantial, and incomes around the higher poverty line are very close together. Differentiating people at this level of income has little validity.

The resumption of economic growth, creating new jobs and generating productivity-based real wage growth would be an effective cure for much of the population in this income range. In addition to benefiting those active in the labor market, it would probably attract discouraged workers back into the workforce, and provide a revenue base for higher pay-as-you-go pensions. Beyond this, however, specific policy interventions in the form of reformed cash transfers could be needed for large families.

*Households with three or more children* are a population group that is over-represented in shallow poverty. This number of children is closely correlated with the low educational level and poor labor-market status of the household head. As such the number of children can also be used as proxy for other variables closely associated with poverty but which may be more difficult as a characteristic for targeting. This interaction between many children in the family, poor educational attainment, and poor labor-market status creates inter-generational poverty. As a poverty group, these households should be high on the priority list of Hungary's policymakers.

*The family allowance* is the main cash transfer program for preventing poverty among children; it has clearly made an important contribution to this goal in recent years. But previous research has shown that the family allowance can do even more, and many recommendations have been forwarded to improve its targeting. (The recommendations have focused on taxing the family allowance, targeting by categorical indicators, using means tests, and applying a combination of these.) This report confirms that the family allowance can play a much more critical role in alleviating poverty. Targeting the family allowance more effectively could virtually eliminate poverty below the higher poverty line.

Measures approved by Parliament in 1995 (Act CXXII) tackle universal entitlement to the family allowance for the first time and attempt to target the transfer to needier households with children. The retention of the family allowance in all families with three and more children is a particularly important feature of the reform, as demonstrated by the simulations in this report. These measures represent a major step forward, but three important problems remain:

- Given the acute problems associated with means testing in Hungary (the data presented in this report bear witness to this problem), and the close proximity of incomes, it is likely that very few households will be excluded from an entitlement on the basis of income (and wealth). As such, budgetary savings will be scant, and will continue to be derived from the loss in real value of the family allowance. (It is quite likely that the cost of administering the means tests will outweigh the financial gains from eliminating a few families.)

- Inflation continues to erode the value of the family allowance, thereby mitigating its role as an anti-poverty instrument for the neediest households. The simulations in this report illustrate the powerful poverty alleviation impact of increasing the real value of the family allowance for families with three or more children. But to afford larger transfers for the neediest families will necessitate finding savings elsewhere. Eliminating eligibility on the basis of easily identifiable characteristics in other selective well-off groups could do the rest.

- There is the so-called "welfare trap". The shift from a universal transfer to a means-tested transfer could act as a disincentive for people to improve their market incomes, since in doing so they might forfeit the family allowance and become worse off (or at least not better off). The sliding scale that determines the withdrawal of the allowance is designed in part to minimize the effect of the welfare trap. How successful it will be will emerge over time. Some modifications might be necessary.

*Helping Those in Deep Poverty*. Among the pockets of deep poverty, one group is particularly vulnerable—the *long-term unemployed*, who have exhausted their wage-related unemployment insurance benefits and have been unable to find a job. It is unlikely that economic growth will lift these people out of poverty without other policy interventions -- this has been the experience of Western Europe. Long-term unemployment is found among prime-age workers (both male and female), the poorly educated, and the unskilled or semi-skilled; it also has strong locational (particularly, in the northeast) and ethnic (gypsy) dimensions. In theory, the long-term unemployed who are active job seekers are entitled to a means-tested social assistance program, introduced in 1993 for this particular target group. Yet the level of payment—up to 80 percent of the minimum pension—is a very modest amount, and quite insufficient to have any meaningful impact on severe poverty. This program needs urgent review. Among other reforms, the level of the transfer should be increased significantly (though not beyond the minimum wage), and wherever possible the payment should be combined with a job-search test, and—as appropriate—active reemployment programs.

*Pensioners* are a particularly important population group in Hungary, numbering almost 3 million. Cash transfers paid as pensions have both a significant absolute and a relative impact on poverty: they keep more than 60 percent of recipient households out of poverty. But this comes at a high cost, currently borne by the working population, and it leaves one group of pensioners -- elderly women -- in deep poverty. While still meeting their other objectives (income smoothing in old-age, and mandatory saving), pensions could be made more effective at combating poverty. One mechanism would be to raise the level of the state-provided minimum pension and ensure that it becomes a genuine minimum—that is no one entitled to a pension would receive less. This scheme could easily be affordable without any additional expenditure if the value of state-provided pensions received by top income households (pensioners) were reduced.

*GYED and GYES* (child care fee and child care allowance) are to be merged in April 1996, and become contingent on means tests, whose income thresholds would be similar to the family allowance. The replacement allowance is to be equal to the minimum pension. The analysis in the report finds women on child care leave among the poorest, and although GYES is one of the most effective programs at reaching the poor, its benefit level is insufficient to lift these families out of poverty. The poverty implications of the proposed changes is not entirely clear, but some negative impact on poverty is likely unless there is a strong labor market response. Some (many?) GYED and GYES recipients will return to work—assuming that they have a job to return to, and someone to take care of their children. In this case, the income/expenditure outcome would be positive. For those who do not (cannot) return to work, the poorly educated and low skilled, the situation could be difficult. This is not to argue against the reform measures, but merely to point out that the situation for some mothers (especially single parents) could deteriorate. Additional interventions might be necessary.

*Reforming the Network of Social Assistance Programs*. According to the analysis in this report, Hungary's social assistance programs are the least effective of all cash transfers at alleviating poverty. Given their function as the last layer of the social safety net, this is a serious failing. Social assistance programs suffer from two major problems:

- They have serious benefit "leakages" and omissions. In part the leakages are a derivative of the high income cut-off for certain programs, but they also reflect the difficulties inherent in means testing, due to the close proximity of incomes, substantial grey and black-economy activities, and other devices to hide income. Omissions are equally serious -- more than 60 percent of households whose income/expenditure is less than the minimum pension do not receive any social assistance payment at all. In part, this may reflect the failure to request social assistance.

- The low level of social assistance payments in general (US$15 monthly per recipient household) and the large variation in payment levels both from one case to another, and from one local authority to another. In particular, the level of payments bear little relationship to need: in some cases, wealthier households receive payments that are larger than those going to poor households. Payments are not always of a regular nature.

The system needs to be overhauled. As elsewhere with the cash transfers system, too many people are currently receiving too little social assistance to ensure any meaningful poverty alleviation where it is most needed.

Some of the shortcomings of the social assistance system are embedded in the design of the 1993 Social Service Welfare Administration and Social Services Act (the Social Act for short). Others arise from inadequate financial resources spent on social assistance, the fragmented nature of programs, and poor administration. There are three basic problems with the 1993 Social Act:

- The income ceiling for some of the social assistance programs is too high. For example, the child-rearing benefit (GYET) has a ceiling of three times the minimum pension per capita. More than 70 percent of the population have an income level below this ceiling.

- Standards that exist for assessing eligibility are based on an inappropriate per capita measure, which does not account for intra-household economies of scale; standards are potentially too generous for large households and discriminate against small households. Some form of equivalence scale should be used as a remedy.

- Many of the social assistance programs do not have a minimum level of support stipulated by law; rather, it is entirely at the discretion of the local governments. There are around 3,200 local governments in Hungary. Some are quite capable of administering the complex social assistance programs, others have neither adequate administrative nor financial capacities. As such, payment levels differ markedly throughout the country.

In addition, the Social Act stopped well short of providing a minimum income for those who are eligible for social assistance. What exists, therefore, is a mixture of some modern, Western approaches to social assistance, overlaid on subjective, case-by-case eligibility criteria that are remnants of the previous system.

Further reform of social assistance programs should capitalize on the experience gained in recent years as well as on the indications on the features of poverty as discussed in this report. In this respect, the categories of citizens entitled to a nationally mandated social assistance program could be extended to include others with a high probability of belonging to poor segments of society. Benefits should then be set at levels ensuring the beneficiaries are lifted above the lowest poverty line, but without creating undue disincentives to work. For example, the elderly without a pension entitlement could be added to the ranks of the long-term unemployed, three-child families, households with large house maintenance costs, and those caring at home for a sick or elderly relative. The system would have to be reasonably coherent and administratively simple so that benefit levels could be made more substantial and the potential target group reached more effectively. At the same time the income ceiling governing eligibility could be lowered. A maximum of twice the minimum pension and possibly only 1.5 times it (preferably on an equivalency rather than per capita basis) would be appropriate.

*Who should assume financing responsibility?* If responsibility for assessing assistance is to remain at the local level - the preferred approach - some of the cost of financing the programs should remain there too. Otherwise, local authorities will have every incentive to accept all claims, since the cost will be entirely met by the center. Yet, giving local authorities too much financial responsibility would continue to prompt local authorities to do their best at minimizing expenditure on social assistance programs. A compromise position should be established, whereby local authorities have incentives to be efficient and effective with social assistance payments, but not frugal to the point of failing to address poverty alleviation. As is the practice in Hungary for support to the long-term unemployed, most countries adopt a cost-sharing arrangement between the local government and the central government. Differential cost-sharing arrangements could be envisaged for different categories of the population—for example, social assistance for the elderly could be reimbursed at a higher percentage than for working age people. But in any event, greater resources in the form of the block grant must be transferred to local governments to enable them to meet their additional funding obligations.

The size and administrative capacity of local governments vary tremendously. Some are quite capable of administering professional programs effectively; others are not. Any policy reform that places more responsibility on the shoulders of local governments should also have measures to strengthen their capacity to administer. In some circumstances, it might make sense to stratify the capacity of local governments and to distribute functions to different levels of government. Personnel should also receive training in modern program operating techniques.

# CHAPTER 1: POVERTY DURING THE TRANSITION

This chapter examines the extent of poverty in Hungary and its distribution by the socioeconomic, demographic, and regional characteristics of households. Its purpose is to provide an in-depth profile of poverty throughout Hungary, as well as an assessment of its determinants. The discussion serves as a prelude to chapter 2, which examines the effectiveness of Hungary's system of cash transfer programs at lifting people out of poverty and providing a safety net for those who remain poor. The report then combines these two discussions into a set of conclusions and policy recommendations for improving the efficiency of poverty alleviation programs, and, more specifically, their eligibility criteria and targeting effectiveness.

The overall message of this report is that poverty during Hungary's economic transition has remained "shallow"—that is, the country's shift to a market-oriented economy has not pushed the majority of the population *too far* below the poverty line. *However, about 5 percent of the population can be considered in "deep poverty"*—benefitting little from Hungary's economic transition nor the programs it has offered to cushion the effects of the transition. As such, despite the apparent effectiveness of Hungary's system of cash transfer programs at supplementing the income of Hungary's population during the transition, the programs targeted specifically at the very poor—the country's "social assistance" programs—are falling short of poverty alleviation objectives.

Before presenting the profile of poverty in Hungary and a discussion of its determinants, the reader should first have a grounding in the concepts and terminology that have provided the basis for analysis throughout this report. The rest of this introduction briefly discusses the key parameters and data sources that are used to measure poverty herein. (Box 1.1 provides a detailed discussion of the rationale for choosing each of these methodological components, and Annex 2 provides further elaboration.)

## Measuring Poverty: More Accurate Definitions

This chapter measures the breadth of poverty in Hungary along two dimensions: the incidence (or "headcount") of poverty, and the poverty gap. The *incidence of poverty* is the proportion of the population who falls below a specified household income or expenditures level that defines a "poverty line." The *poverty gap* is the average "shortfall" of household income or expenditures as a percentage of the poverty line.

Hungary, however, does not have an official or even widely used poverty-line benchmark. Rather, various benchmarks are available, each of which provides merely a piece of the poverty profile. In Hungary, two types of poverty lines are used: an absolute line, the minimum pension; and relative proportions of mean household income or expenditure (half of mean, and two-thirds of mean). At the same time, an assessment of whether a household is in poverty can be based alternatively on its income or its expenditures—each of which yields slightly different poverty "headcounts." In addition, two household data sources for assessing poverty are available in Hungary—the 1993 Household Budget Survey, and the 1992-93-94 Household Panel Survey. Again, each yields different estimates of the extent of poverty in Hungary. To ensure more consistent and precise results, the analysis presented in this report relies primarily on the following parameters:[1]

---

[1]    Again, the rationale of choosing these parameters, as well as the shortcomings of the alternatives, is described in Box 1.1, and Annex 2.

---

**Box 1.1: The Definitions and Data Sources Used in the Report**

Poverty lines. Hungary does not have an official or even widely used poverty line. In the past, the **subsistence minima** was widely used. The usefulness of the subsistence minimum for poverty analysis has been reduced over time, and in recent times the CSO has suspended its calculation. The reason is that the calculation method of this minimum pre-dates the economic transition, when the relative prices of goods were different from what they are now. In 1993, the real value of the subsistence minimum had increased to a point where is was barely below average household expenditure for the country (the latter being the equivalent of US$166 per month) thereby classifying more than 50 percent of the population as "poor". Clearly, this makes it difficult to interpret as a genuine "subsistence minimum", meaning that those below it live in absolute poverty.

Within the benchmarks utilized in the social transfer system, only the **minimum pension** has a poverty connotation, as it implies the minimum sum of money needed for a single retired adult to live on. It is also used as the basis for various social assistance programs. In 1993, the minimum pension was, on average, 6,400 HUF/month (US$70). The minimum pension in 1993 was worth only 73 percent of its real 1989 value. This poverty line can be used to identify the very poorest individuals in Hungary in 1993.

There is a strong tradition in Hungary of using **relative poverty lines**—lines derived from the data themselves. Relative poverty analysis often uses a set fraction (1/3, 1/2, 2/3) of mean income/expenditure as a poverty benchmark. This analysis uses both half and two-thirds of the mean as poverty lines. Since both these lines fall between the minimum pension and the subsistence minimum they serve as a useful device for showing the sensitivity of poverty estimates to the poverty line selected

Data sources. This study utilizes two household data sources: the 1993 Household Budget Survey (HBS); and the 1992-93-94 Household Panel Survey (HPS). The 1993 HBS, which is the main data source, is part of a tradition of budget surveys undertaken by the Central Statistical Office (CSO) since the early 1950s. The surveys are conducted every two years, and 1993 is the first HBS which fully incorporates western economic concepts. The 1993 sample is about 9,000 households, selected in a two-stage stratified design, and covering the whole non-institutional population in Hungary. Although not possible to quantify, the HBS probably fails to capture some of the very poorest, namely the homeless. This is a common problem with income/expenditure surveys. The HPS's main advantage is that it follows the same households over time, thus permitting study of the dynamics of poverty. It is this feature of the data which is utilized in this report. The drawback is that the sample size is only 2,000 households, so that the amount of disaggregation in the analysis is limited.

Income versus expenditure. Most previous work on poverty and social transfers in Hungary has relied on income (for example, see Szivos 1994; Toth et al 1994; Milanovic 1991). The main reason was the high quality of income data in past Hungarian household surveys. This study breaks with that tradition, using **household expenditures as the basis for analysis** for two reasons:

- There are strong and well-known theoretical advantages to using household expenditures for poverty analysis, because they reflect permanent income more effectively(for example, see Deaton and Muelbauer 1980).

- The weight of evidence, from the 1993 HBS and the earlier HBS, suggests that the reporting problems are more severe with income. This pertains especially to private sector income, and the incomes of the self-employed and sole proprietors.

Using household expenditures rather than household income as the basis for the poverty calculations and the incidence of cash transfers will yield different results. As indicated in Table 1.2, the poverty incidence (poverty headcount) is higher on the basis of expenditure data. This is well illustrated in Figure 1.2. Up to a poverty line of HUF 200,000 yearly (HUF 16,667 monthly), the selection of expenditure as the criterion will lead to higher poverty estimates than if income is selected. Another important feature is that households are ranked differently by the two different distributions. At the same time, using household expenditures as the basis to measure the well-being of households requires that household size and composition be taken into account. This is done by expressing expenditures on a **per adult equivalent basis**. The OECD-scale has been used (first adult=1; other adults=0.7; children less than 14 years=0.5). This scale corresponds closely to the one implicit in the calculation of subsistence minimums by the CSO for different types of households.

- *Poverty lines*
  - A minimum pension to identify the very poorest individuals in Hungary. For comparative purposes, in this opening chapter, the 1989 minimum pension is used. For the bulk of the analysis later in the report, the 1993 actual current value is used;
  - Half of mean household income to demonstrate poverty trends between 1989 and 1993; and
  - Two-thirds of mean *household expenditures* to identify those who are in "shallow" poverty in 1993.

- *Household expenditures*, rather than income, are used as the basis for the poverty profile in the body of the report.[2]

- The analysis relies primarily on the 1993 Household Budget Survey (HBS). The HBS is part of a tradition of budget surveys undertaken by the Central Statistical Office (CSO) since the early 1950's. A secondary household data set is the 1992-93-94 Household Panel Survey (HPS), which is a survey conducted by TARKI (the Social Research Informatics Center).

## The Incidence of Poverty and the Poverty Gap: Dynamic and Static Implications

From 1989 to 1993, the incidence of poverty increased substantially for each poverty line used in this report—the proportion of households with income below the minimum pension increased from 1.6 percent in 1989 to 8.6 percent in 1993; and the proportion of households with income at *half* of mean household income increased from 4.3 percent in 1989 to 34.6 percent in 1993 (Table 1.1 and Figure 1.1). It is quite likely that these estimates overstate the increase in poverty incidence due to the under-reporting of income in 1993.[3]

But large increases in the incidence of poverty are not unexpected, for two reasons. First, the poverty gap indicates that poverty in Hungary has remained "shallow"—that is, despite a greater number of households in poverty, the average income (or expenditures) of the poor has not fallen *substantially* below the exact poverty lines. The poverty gap between 1989 and 1993 has ranged from 15 to 20 percent; and for each poverty line, it has actually declined over the period. In contrast, the poverty incidence rates for each line has widened considerably. This disparity is not surprising because many of the households with incomes close to the poverty lines have fallen just below them, indicating, again, the existence of "shallow" poverty. But a closer examination of the comparative poverty gap and incidence rates shows that Hungary does have specific "deep pockets of poverty"—the very poor, who are not being captured or targeted effectively by poverty alleviation interventions.

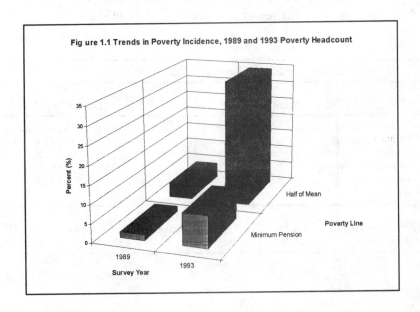

Fig ure 1.1 Trends in Poverty Incidence, 1989 and 1993 Poverty Headcount

---

[2]    Income, however, is used for comparative analysis with HBS from earlier years. (Table 1.1)

[3]    The distribution of unreported income is unknown. It is thought that income derived from the informal economy is a distorted "U curve", with some unrecorded income in the lowest decile, but most in the upper deciles.

| Table 1.1: The Incidence of Poverty and the Poverty Gap: 1989 and 1993 (1989 values) | | | | |
|---|---|---|---|---|
| | Poverty Headcount | | Poverty Gap | |
| | 1989 | 1993 | 1989 | 1993 |
| **Poverty line:** *(1989 values, held constant)* | (%) | (%) | (%) | (%) |
| Minimum pension | 1.6 | 8.6 | 20.8 | 15.8 |
| Half of mean | 4.3 | 34.6 | 17.1 | 15.6 |

Source: Szivos, Peter. "Evolution of Poverty in Hungary, 1987-1992", CSO, Budapest, November 1994; and World Bank calculations for 1993.
Notes: The 1993 poverty lines in 1989 constant value were calculated by inflating the 1989 values (minimum pension = 3490 Ft/month: US$59; half of mean = 4897 Ft/month: US$83) by the CPI. Estimates are derived from income data in the Household Budget Surveys for 1989 and 1993.

Second, the contrast between substantial increases in the incidence of poverty and only small poverty gaps is due to the concentration of some 75 to 80 percent of the population in a very narrow income range (Figure 1.2). Small declines in income (or expenditures)—due either to income underreporting in surveys or real income declines—can lead to huge jumps in the number of people who fall below a given poverty line. Table 1.2 illustrates this problem well by showing the incidence of poverty when 1993 current values (rather than 1989 constant values) of the same two poverty lines (plus one additional line) are applied to the same 1993 HBS. A relatively small change in the value of the poverty line increases the incidence of poverty by quite a large amount. This table also illustrates the variation in poverty incidence when using household expenditure rather than household income as the basis for the calculations. The implications of using expenditure based estimates, and 1993 current values for the poverty line throughout much of this report should thus be kept in mind.

| Table 1.2: The Incidence of Poverty in 1993 (1993 values) | | |
|---|---|---|
| | Expenditure based (%) | Income based (%) |
| **Poverty line:** *(1993 values)* | | |
| Minimum pension | 4.5 | 2.5 |
| Half of mean | 9.3 | 5.0 |
| Two thirds of mean | 25.3 | 17.0 |

Note: Poverty lines have the following forint monthly values: minimum pension, HUF 6,400; half mean, HUF 7,597; two-thirds of mean, HUF 10,129.

**Figure 1.2: Concentration of Income and Expenditures Among the Population: 1989 and 1993**

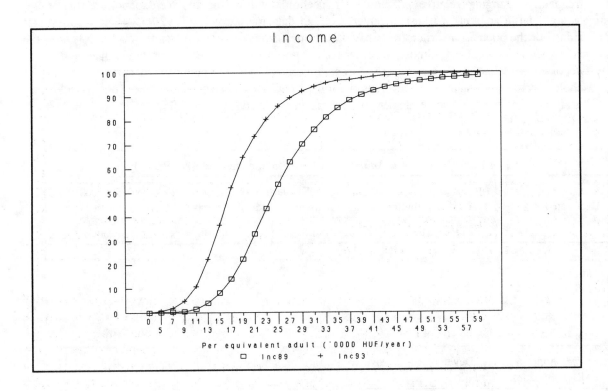

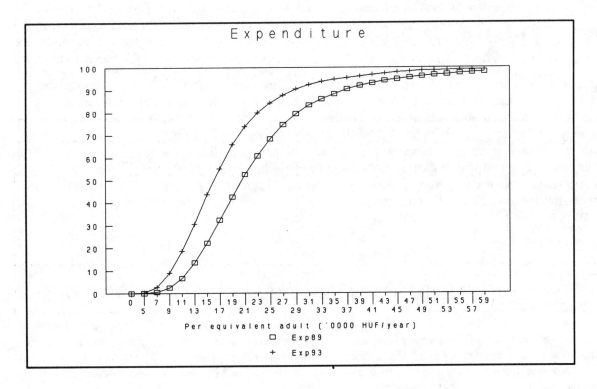

Another dimension of the picture of poverty that emerges in Hungary in the transitional years is the frequently changing relative position of households within the income/expenditure hierarchy, suggesting a large amount of transient poverty. Panel data for the years 1992-93-94 show substantial "churning" of the population, whereby relative positions change quite dramatically from one year to the next. Between 1993 and 1994, almost 40 percent of the population changed their relative income position by two or more deciles. This is thought to occur because of the irregularity of certain elements of household income. Of concern, however, is the lowest decile, where movement was considerably less, indicating the emergence of some element of "permanent poverty" (Table 1.3).[4]

| Table 1.3: Movement of Individuals Between Income Deciles, 1993-94 | | | | |
|---|---|---|---|---|
| Decile in 1993 | Decile in 1994 (% distribution of individuals in 1994 deciles compared to 1993 position) | | | |
| | Poorest | 2nd-5th | 6th-9th | Richest |
| Poorest | 59.4 | 35.9 | 4.5 | 1.6 |
| 2nd-5th | 32.7 | 36.4 | 24.1 | 5.0 |
| 6th-9th | 7.0 | 21.6 | 33.6 | 38.2 |
| Richest | 0.9 | 6.1 | 37.8 | 55.2 |
| Total | 100.0 | 100.0 | 100.0 | 100.0 |
| *Source*: Andorka et.al. "Development in Poverty and Income Inequalities in Hungary 1992-1994". TARKI, Budapest, April 1995. | | | | |

## Why Has Poverty Increased in Hungary?

Two factors increase the extent of poverty in a country: a decline in overall income, and a more unequal distribution of income levels. Both trends have been documented for the transitional countries of Central and Eastern Europe. (Milanovic 1995) In Hungary, a decline in measured real household income is primarily responsible for the rise in the incidence of poverty;[5] because household incomes are densely concentrated just above and below all the poverty lines, even a small decline in income levels can lead to a substantial increase in the incidence of poverty. But growing income inequality in Hungary—largely a disparate distribution of the national decline in overall income—has also played a part in the rising incidence of poverty. Indeed, the poorest 10 percent of the population have suffered the largest decline in real income; in contrast, the richest decile have actually had real income gains. (Figure 1.4)

---

[4] Further analysis of the three year data in the HPS found around 3 percent of the population in poverty in all years (1992-93-94).

[5] The magnitude of the *measured* income decline varies between data sources; for example, household survey data show a more significant decline than national accounts data—27 percent versus 11 percent. But note that incomes in the 1993 HBS are under-reported by around 38 percent, and that consumption is under-reported by around 32 percent when compared to national accounts data (Szivos 1995).

*A Decline in Income.* Hungary's recession since the collapse of the old order broadly mirrors the contractions in aggregate output and income observed throughout Central Europe.[6] Between 1989-93, Hungary's (real) GDP fell by an estimated 18 percent, and unemployment, which stood at 28,500 at the end of 1989, peaked in the first quarter of 1993 at almost 700,000—13.5 percent of the labor force. Although recovery on both fronts began in 1994, when GDP increased (at an estimated 2.9 percent) for the first time in five years and when registered unemployment fell back to 12 percent of the labor force, formal sector employment, particularly in agriculture, mining, and heavy industry, has continued its precipitous decline. The decline reflects not only the large number of unemployed, but also growing labor force inactivity (a withdrawal from the labor force of almost 10 percent in 5 years). Workers have opted to take various pension arrangements (disability and early retirement), withdraw voluntarily from work, rely heavily on programs that remove them from registered unemployment and thus work-search rules (for example, extended maternity/child care programs), and engage in informal sector work activity. But while formal employment has declined during the economic transition, real wages have remained fairly robust, despite steep declines during the inflationary period of 1989-91. As such, both national accounts and household survey data indicate that the decline in labor-generated household income during 1989-93 reflects shrinking employment (that is, rising unemployment and labor-force inactivity), rather than any significant decline in real wages.[7] At the same time, the level of private domestic consumption has fallen, but less than the decline in labor-generated disposable income due to a fairly steady level of cash transfer payments to households (from, again, pension arrangements, the unemployment program, child care allowance, and sick leave). The interaction of all these forces as they affect the decline in measured real income is displayed graphically in Figure 1.3 (and Table 1.4).

| Table 1.4: Key Economic Indicators 1989-94 | | | | | | | |
|---|---|---|---|---|---|---|---|
| | 1989 | 1990 | 1991 | 1992 | 1993 | 1994 | 1989-93 |
| Percentage (real) change over previous year | | | | | | | |
| GDP | -0.2 | -3.5 | -11.9 | -3.0 | -0.8 | 2.9 | -18.0 |
| Private consumption | n.a. | -3.6 | -5.8 | -0.5 | 1.3 | 0.7 | -10.6 |
| Disposable money income (net) | 3.0 | -2.6 | -4.3 | -3.3 | -6.2 | 3.6 | -10.5 |
| Labor income (gross) | 0.4 | -2.9 | -11.7 | -4.6 | -4.6 | -0.9 | -17.4 |
| Cash transfers (gross) | 7.3 | -2.9 | 0.7 | 4.1 | -2.4 | -1.0 | 0.0 |
| Employment | -0.5 | -0.6 | -3.2 | -10.6 | -10.2 | -3.6 | -20.9 |
| Real wages | 0.9 | -3.7 | -4.0 | 1.4 | -0.8 | 3.1 | -7.2 |
| Annual rate | | | | | | | |
| Unemployment Rates | 0.6 | 0.7 | 3.0 | 9.6 | 13.5 | 12.0 | |
| *Source*: Central Statistical Office and Ministry of Finance. | | | | | | | |

---

[6] The World Bank's latest country economic memorandum, "Hungary: Structural Reforms and Sustainable Growth," June 1995 provides an in-depth discussion of Hungary's recent economic developments.

[7] One of the adverse budgetary consequences of the absence of any major real wage decline is the perpetuation of the value of social cash transfers, since the bulk of (social-based) cash transfer (pensions, sick pay, maternity and child care, and unemployment benefit) are pegged to wages at their point of establishment. Only with time and inflation does the real value of transfers decline, when transfers are not (fully) indexed to the CPI.

**Figure 1.3:  Key Economic Indicators: 1988-94**

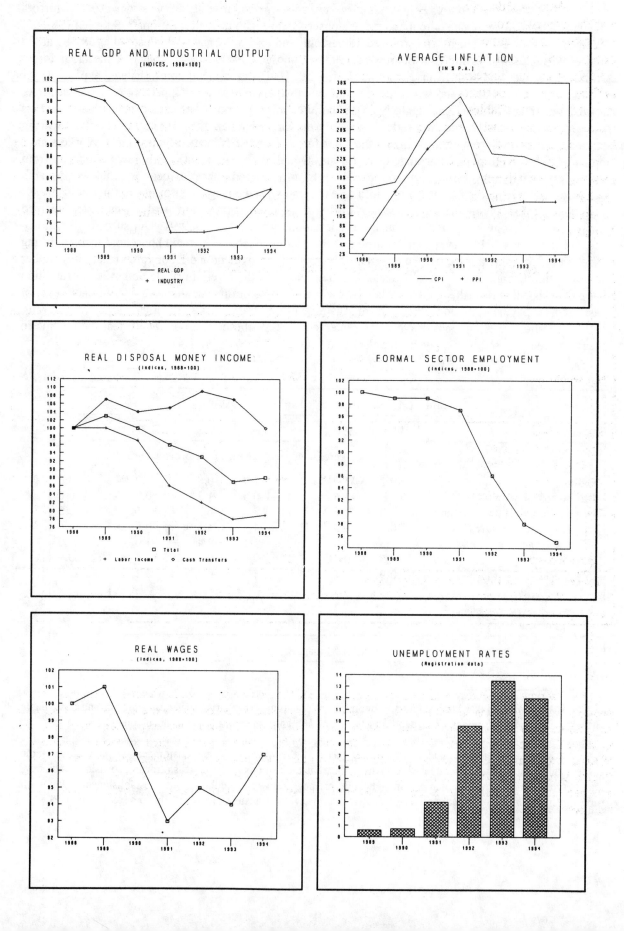

Household data corroborate national accounts data on the declining role of labor-generated income and the increasing role of cash transfer payments.[8] During 1989-93, labor income fell by between 17 and 30 percent in real terms (depending on the source), and its share in gross household income fell from 68 percent to 65 percent. In contrast, cash transfers income lost little of its real value, and its share in gross household income increased from 28 percent in 1989 to almost 31 percent in 1993 (Table 1.5). The shifting relative importance of labor income and social income has affected different population groups in different ways (Tables 1.5). Basically, households that have relied heavily on insurance-based cash transfers, such as pension recipients, have improved their relative standing, due in part to the relationship between benefits and (real) wages. The losers have been those who have lost their relationship with the labor market, as well as those who have relied heavily on cash transfers that have not maintained their real value (for example, the family allowance and social assistance). However, average (adjusted per capita) household income is still higher in those households in which the ratio of active earners to dependents (children, inactive workers, and elderly) is greatest. But the gap among all household groups has closed.

| Table 1.5: Trends in Household Income from Labor and Cash Transfers: 1989-93[*] | | | | | | | |
|---|---|---|---|---|---|---|---|
| | Share of Household Income from: | | | | | | |
| | Labor income (%) | | Social (cash transfers) income (%) | | Decline in real value 1989-93 (%) | | |
| Household type | 1989 | 1993 | 1989 | 1993 | Labor income | Social Income | All income |
| Single person | 88.3 | 80.4 | 11.7 | 19.6 | 33.2 | 12.2 | 30.4 |
| Single (elderly) person | 11.4 | 7.2 | 88.6 | 92.8 | 46.3 | 11.1 | 17.0 |
| 1 adult, 1 + child(ren) | 60.7 | 63.1 | 39.3 | 36.9 | 23.6 | 31.0 | 22.0 |
| 2 adults | 55.4 | 45.0 | 44.6 | 55.0 | 38.7 | 6.8 | 25.5 |
| 2 adults, 1 or 2 child(ren) | 81.1 | 77.3 | 18.9 | 22.7 | 31.8 | 14.5 | 29.0 |
| 2 adults, 3 + children | 63.9 | 58.3 | 36.1 | 41.7 | 33.4 | 15.5 | 27.7 |
| Other | 77.5 | 72.2 | 22.5 | 27.8 | 30.3 | 7.1 | 27.6 |
| All households | 68.0 | 65.3 | 28.2 | 30.8 | 30.5 | 12.1 | 26.9[**] |

Source: 1989 and 1993 HBS, CSO Budapest.
Notes: *Excludes private transfers and "other" income. **The decline in real household expenditures for the same period is 18.5 percent.

[8] A serious omission in both the national accounts and household data should be stressed at this point. Neither captures income generated in the hidden (grey and black) economy. Estimates of the size of this hidden economy vary, but the most precisely calculated estimate indicates that official GDP figures underreport the size of this sector by about 20 percent (Arvay and Vertes 1993). The same study shows a growing hidden economy throughout the 1980s and the early 1990s. Although not possible to quantify, the impact of the hidden economy on household income is likely to be one of cushioning. Sik (unpublished) finds that income from the grey economy shows a distorted "U" curve, with some informal sector income being captured by the poorest decile but most accruing to the upper deciles.

*Growing Income Disparity.* Within the confines of data limitations, all indications are that the distribution of household income has become more unequal during the transition. This trend was already beginning in Hungary in the 1980s, when the Gini coefficient increased by 3 points within five years, when the share of income accruing to the poorest decile declined and the share to the wealthiest decile increased. The trend has apparently been continued to the present time. In 1989 the ratio of expenditures by the wealthiest and poorest deciles was 3 to 1: by 1993, it has increased to 5.3 to 1 (Figure 1.4). (The expenditure ratio between the wealthiest 5 percent compared to the poorest 5 percent was 7.5 to 1 in 1993). For the middle 20-80 percent of the income decile range, the decline in real expenditures is comparatively equal; the income disparity between the lowest and highest 20 percent is enormous (bottom of Figure 1.4).

*Disparities in Sources of Income.* Much of the reason for the unequal distribution of income among income groups in Hungary—and thus for the increase in the incidence of poverty—can be seen in the distribution of income <u>sources</u> among the population.

### Figure 1.4: Growing Expenditure Inequality during the Transition

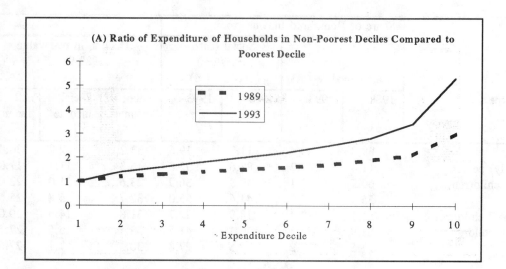

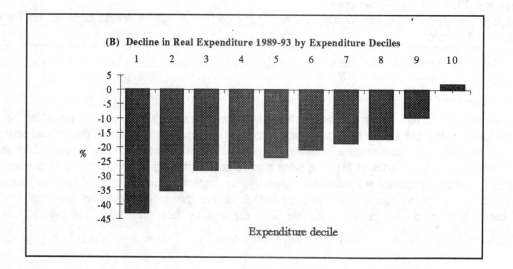

Primarily earned income (wages, self-employment, business, and property) accounts for an average of 65 percent of disposable household income, with tremendous variation among households. The poorest households (those below the minimum pension) derive only one-third of their income from market sources, relying heavily on cash transfer payments—pensions, unemployment benefits, the family allowance, and social assistance. In contrast, the wealthier households derive more than two-thirds of their income from market sources; but they also derive around 20 percent of their income from social transfer (Figure 1.5). <u>But this wealthier group of households receives almost the same nominal value of social cash transfers as do the poorest households (which is indeed also true of the households in the two middle categories do as well)</u>. As such, <u>income earned from market activities is the primary determinant of where a household is ranked in the income spectrum</u>. As discussed in the remainder of this chapter, several factors affect access to market income: age (new entrants to the labor market and those close to and above retirement age are less inclined to be active in the labor market); level of education and skill

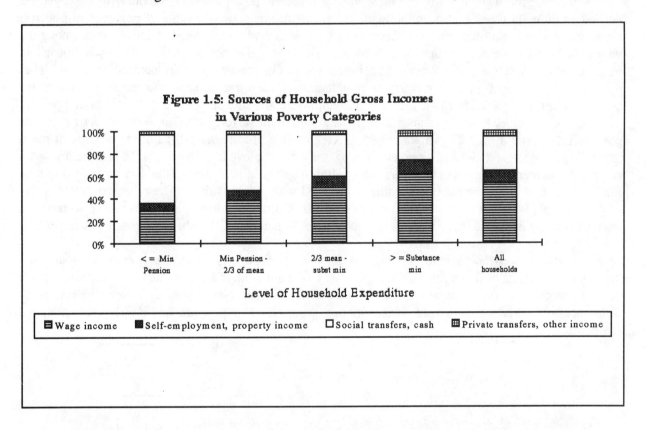

**Figure 1.5: Sources of Household Gross Incomes in Various Poverty Categories**

(which affect both the probability of having a regular job and wage-earning potential);[9] and location (proximity to the major employment centers increases wage-earning potential). Households that have business interests and/or property are doing relatively well (Annex Table A3.2).

---

[9]   Earnings data by level of education show increasing returns to secondary and higher education. For example, the wages of university graduates in the competitive sphere of the Hungarian economy have increased from a factor of 2.10 in 1989 to 2.52 in 1994 when compared with the wages of workers with a secondary education.

## A Profile of Poverty in Hungary

The rest of this chapter provides a disaggregated analysis of the incidence of poverty throughout Hungary. It assesses the distribution of poverty among Hungarian households by three broad socioeconomic and demographic categories: the income earning status of the head of household; the composition of households, as well as the education and age of the household head; and region of the country in which households are located. This breakdown provides the essential components of the distribution of poverty in Hungary, serving as an analytical foundation for chapter 2, which discusses whether the country's cash transfer system is targeting groups of the poor effectively.

*Poverty and Income-Earning Status.* The incidence of poverty varies widely across socioeconomic groups (Figure 1.6).[10] Households whose head is unemployed, temporarily employed, or dependent on child care benefits as the main source of income show the highest incidence of poverty. On average, about one-fifth of these households are below the minimum pension and are thus among the very poorest in Hungary; more than 50 percent are below the higher poverty line (2/3 of mean household expenditures). Pensioners also show a higher-than-average incidence of poverty according to the higher poverty line. The incidence of poverty is lowest among the three groups with economically active household heads: permanent employees, the self-employed, and sole proprietors.[11] Only about 2 percent of these three socioeconomic groups fall below the minimum poverty line on average; yet the higher poverty line shows a wide disparity: only 5 percent of sole proprietors fall below two-thirds of mean expenditures, compared with 23 percent among the self-employed. Clearly, sole proprietors, who comprise 1 percent of the population, are the wealthiest group in Hungary. They have managed to take full advantage of the economic opportunities associated with the transition. The other extreme consists of those people who in a sense are the victims of the transition: the unemployed and those with only a tenuous connection to the labor market, who comprise 30 percent of the absolute poor (Figure 1.7).

Because households with the highest incidence of poverty (temporary employees and the unemployed) also have the largest poverty gaps, they face a double jeopardy: they have the highest risk of being poor, and their poverty is deeper than that of other poor groups. Nevertheless, these differences in poverty gaps across socioeconomic groups in Hungary are not large by international standards.[12]

---

[10] The socioeconomic categories are based on the income-earning status of the head of household, implying some limitations with the categorization. For example, unemployed people are found throughout all socioeconomic groups, not only among the "unemployed" head of household group. Similarly, employed persons can be found in pensioner households and vice versa.

[11] Self-employed are defined as those who work for their own account; sole proprietors own enterprises that also hire other employees.

[12] Yet they are larger than those in some other economies in transition, such as Poland.

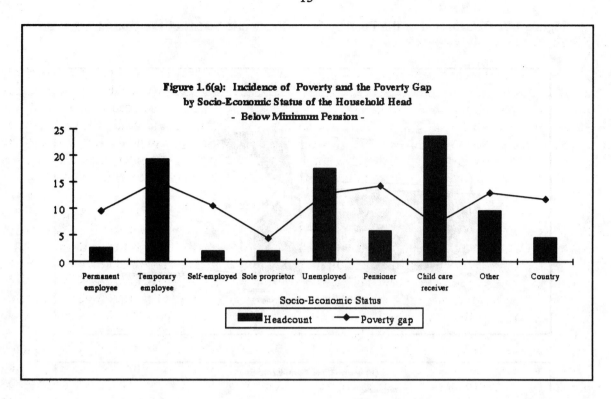

Figure 1.6(a): Incidence of Poverty and the Poverty Gap
by Socio-Economic Status of the Household Head
- Below Minimum Pension -

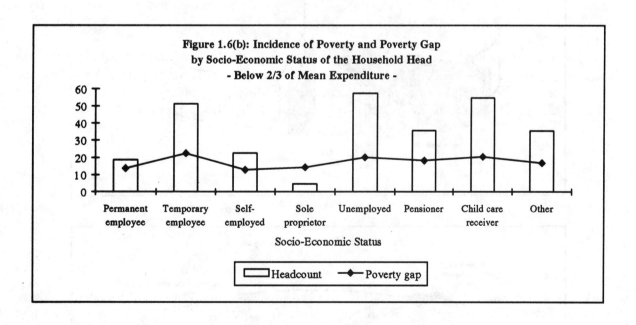

Figure 1.6(b): Incidence of Poverty and Poverty Gap
by Socio-Economic Status of the Household Head
- Below 2/3 of Mean Expenditure -

## Figure 1.7: Distribution of the Poor by Socio-Economic Status of the Household Head

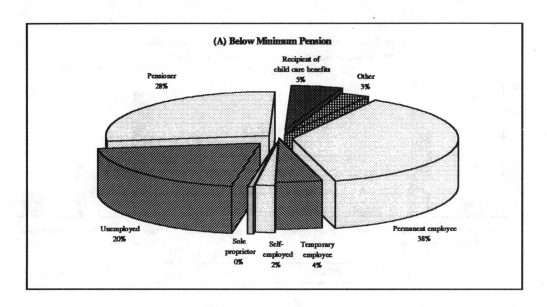

**(A) Below Minimum Pension**

Pensioner 28%

Recipient of child care benefits 5%

Other 3%

Unemployed 20%

Sole proprietor 0%

Self-employed 2%

Temporary employee 4%

Permanent employee 38%

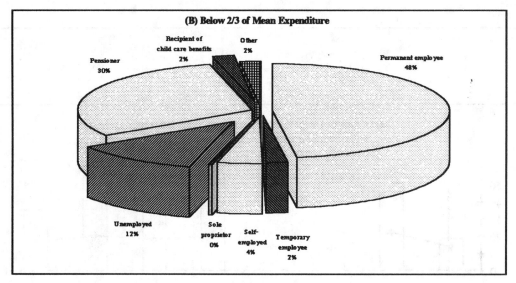

**(B) Below 2/3 of Mean Expenditure**

Recipient of child care benefits 2%

Other 2%

Pensioner 30%

Permanent employee 48%

Unemployed 12%

Sole proprietor 0%

Self-employed 4%

Temporary employee 2%

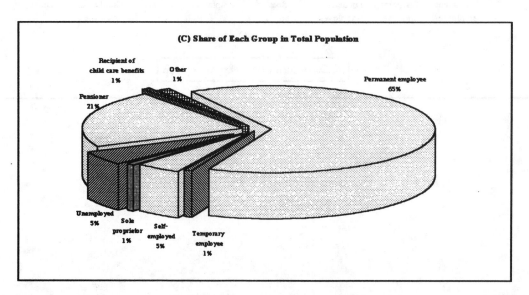

**(C) Share of Each Group in Total Population**

Recipient of child care benefits 1%

Other 1%

Pensioner 21%

Permanent employee 65%

Unemployed 5%

Sole proprietor 1%

Self-employed 5%

Temporary employee 1%

*Poverty and the Labor Market.* The preceding section highlights the link between labor market attachment and poverty status. Although a thorough investigation of this link falls outside the scope of this report, the role of unemployment as a determinant of poverty is important to the analysis in this chapter. Unemployment is a recent phenomenon in Hungary, and its rapid emergence is one of the key reasons for the increased incidence of poverty. Unemployment pervades almost every socioeconomic group in Hungary: 15 to 19 percent of households whose head is actively employed contain an unemployed member, and 1 to 2 percent contain two or more unemployed members. The incidence of unemployment is much higher in households whose head is unemployed, or depends on child care benefits as the main source of income. The coverage of unemployment benefits was quite high at the time of the HBS: 76 percent of households with one unemployed member received unemployment insurance, as did 88 percent of those with multiple unemployed members. (Table 1.6) Such high coverage would be less today for two reasons. The duration of benefits has been shortened to one year, and the proportion of unemployed who are long-term unemployed has increased.

| Table 1.6: Income-Earning Status of Household Head and Unemployment | | | | |
|---|---|---|---|---|
| Income-earning status | Households without unemployed member | Households with 1 unemployed member | Households with 2 or more unemployed members | Total |
| Permanent employee | 83.5% | 14.9% | 1.6% | 100.0% |
| Temporary employee | 83.8% | 15.4% | 0.8% | 100.0% |
| Self-employed | 80.6% | 19.2% | 0.2% | 100.0% |
| Sole proprietor | 81.9% | 18.1% | 0.0% | 100.0% |
| Unemployed | 0.0% | 70.4% | 29.6% | 100.0% |
| Pensioner | 94.1% | 4.9% | 1.0% | 100.0% |
| Child care benefits recipient | 63.4% | 29.7% | 6.9% | 100.0% |
| Other | 84.8% | 14.1% | 1.1% | 100.0% |
| Country | 83.2% | 14.2% | 2.6% | 100.0% |
| Percent receiving unemployment benefits | 3.7%[a] | 76.2% | 88.5% | |

[a] Some households without unemployed members receive benefits because the HBS uses a longer reference period for income sources than for the determination of unemployment status.

Several observations can be made about the relationship between the incidence of poverty and whether or not the household head is unemployed, the number of unemployed household members, and whether or not the household receives unemployment insurance benefits (Table 1.7). First, the incidence of poverty is higher if the household head is unemployed than if another household member is unemployed. Second, if the head is unemployed, unemployment insurance benefits represent a very important source of income. In households that do not receive unemployment insurance benefits, including those whole eligibility has expired, up to 40 percent with unemployed heads fall below the

| Table 1.7: Poverty Incidence and Poverty Gap by Unemployment Characteristics | | | | |
|---|---|---|---|---|
| | Below minimum pension | | Below 2/3 of mean expenditure | |
| | Headcount | Poverty gap | Headcount | Poverty gap |
| Unemployed head, 1 unemployed member, benefits | 16.6% | 10.8% | 56.8% | 20.0% |
| Unemployed head, 1 unemployed member, no benefits | 40.3% | 14.2% | 52.1% | 31.3% |
| Unemployed head, 2+ unemployed members, benefits | 12.4% | 17.7% | 59.7% | 17.7% |
| Unemployed head, 2+ unemployed members, no benefits | 41.4% | 9.5% | 52.7% | 29.4% |
| Employed head, 0 unemployed members, benefits | 0.5% | 22.2% | 20.3% | 12.8% |
| Employed head, 0 unemployed members, no benefits | 2.7% | 11.1% | 20.6% | 15.1% |
| Employed head, 1 unemployed member, benefits | 4.4% | 10.4% | 30.5% | 14.7% |
| Employed head, 1 unemployed member, no benefits | 14.8% | 10.3% | 43.2% | 20.1% |
| Employed head, 2+ unemployed members, benefits | 22.1% | 14.4% | 62.6% | 20.9% |
| Employed head, 2+ unemployed members, no benefits | 22.2% | 15.3% | 51.5% | 23.3% |
| All | 4.5% | 11.7% | 25.3% | 16.2% |

Note: **Headcount of poverty** is the percentage of people below the poverty line; **poverty gap** is the average shortfall of household expenditure per equivalent adult as a percentage of the poverty line.

minimum pension poverty line—more than three times more than among households that receive unemployment insurance benefits. Although their number is small in absolute terms, households headed by an unemployed person and which do not receive unemployment insurance benefits have the highest incidence of poverty of any classification. Third, if the household head is employed, the incidence of poverty rises with the number of unemployed household members, but the effect of unemployment insurance benefits on poverty alleviation is less pronounced.

*Poverty and Region of Country*. The regional variation in the incidence of poverty is much less pronounced than among socioeconomic groups. Budapest has the lowest incidence of poverty, while the predominantly rural North and South Plains have the highest incidence (Table 1.8). This disparity is consistent with the finding that poverty is deeper in villages than in cities, which in turn reflects variations in employment opportunities and the informal economy. The incidence of poverty in all other regions is similar for both poverty lines, suggesting that region is not a very important target for poverty alleviation policy in Hungary. The poverty gap shows the same pattern as the headcount pattern, with one exception: Pest County has the highest poverty gap, despite having a slightly lower than average incidence of poverty. It appears that this area, which surrounds the capital city, contains few pockets of relatively deep poverty. This issue may need to be investigated further.

| Table 1.8: Incidence of Poverty and Poverty Gap by Region | | | | | |
|---|---|---|---|---|---|
| | Below minimum pension (%) | | Below 2/3 of mean expenditure (%) | | Share of each region in total population (%) |
| Region | Headcount | Poverty gap | Headcount | Poverty gap | |
| Budapest | 2.7 | 9.7 | 21.1 | 14.9 | 19.5 |
| Pest County | 4.2 | 15.0 | 23.7 | 17.2 | 9.3 |
| North Hungary | 4.1 | 13.7 | 25.6 | 16.0 | 12.6 |
| North Plain | 6.0 | 11.0 | 31.9 | 16.9 | 14.9 |
| South Plain | 6.0 | 11.2 | 28.2 | 17.1 | 13.4 |
| West Transdanubia | 4.2 | 12.6 | 23.4 | 16.4 | 9.7 |
| North Transdanubia | 4.8 | 10.6 | 23.7 | 16.2 | 10.8 |
| South Transdanubia | 4.2 | 11.4 | 24.4 | 15.1 | 9.8 |
| Towns* | 3.7 | 10.6 | 23.6 | 15.3 | |
| Villages | 6.2 | 12.8 | 29.2 | 17.5 | |
| All Hungary | 4.5 | 11.7 | 25.3 | 16.2 | 100.0 |
| Note: *Towns other than Budapest. | | | | | |

*Poverty and Household Characteristics*. Demographic characteristics—the number of adults and children and the gender of the head of household—are important indicators of poverty in Hungary.

Poverty is lowest in nuclear households with 1 or 2 children (Table 1.9 and Figure 1.8). The incidence of poverty is similar among households of childless couples or single adults (many of whom are pensioners). Poverty rises steadily with the number of children, and is especially high among households with 2 adults and 4 or more children, and in households with 3 or more adults and 3 or more children. Among those households, one in five live below the minimum pension, and more than 70 percent live below 2/3 of mean expenditures. It is noteworthy, however, that the poverty gap among these households is not abnormally high (Table 1.9). The largest poverty gap occurs among single adults. Although single adults comprise only 6.5 percent of the population and do not suffer from a high incidence of poverty, they do contain a pocket of deeper than average poverty.

Hungary exhibits a distinct gender dimension to poverty (Table 1.9), with a higher incidence of poverty among female-headed households. Among one-person households, the difference is particularly pronounced at the higher poverty line (2/3 of mean expenditures). Many of these female-headed households are widowed pensioners living alone. Poverty is also above average among single adults with children, the majority of whom are women. Of course, such aggregate figures mask many different situations facing women as they access the labor market and the social transfers system.

**Table 1.9: The Incidence of Poverty and the Poverty Gap by Household Composition and Gender of Household Head**

| | Poverty line | | | | Share of each category in total population |
| | Below minimum pension | | Below 2/3 of mean expenditures | | |
| | Headcount | Poverty gap | Headcount | Poverty gap | |
|---|---|---|---|---|---|
| **Household composition** | | | | | |
| 1 male | 4.8% | 12.9% | 22.6% | 21.1% | 1.4% |
| 1 female | 5.3% | 15.6% | 34.7% | 19.5% | 5.1% |
| 1 adult with children | 9.2% | 9.5% | 24.9% | 19.0% | 2.0% |
| 2+ adults | 3.3% | 12.4% | 22.5% | 16.4% | 42.6% |
| 2 adults with 1-2 children | 2.8% | 12.2% | 20.4% | 14.4% | 26.9% |
| 2 adults with 3 children | 6.4% | 7.8% | 29.8% | 13.7% | 3.6% |
| 2 adults with 4+ children | 19.0% | 11.1% | 71.4% | 14.5% | 1.3% |
| 3+ adults with 1-2 children | 6.5% | 10.6% | 29.4% | 15.8% | 15.5% |
| 3+ adults with 3+ children | 21.4% | 11.6% | 72.7% | 21.2% | 1.4% |
| **Gender** | | | | | |
| Male-headed household | 3.8% | 11.6% | 23.7% | 15.8% | 77.0% |
| Female-headed household | 6.5% | 11.9% | 30.8% | 17.4% | 23.0% |
| **All** | 4.5% | 11.7% | 25.3% | 16.2% | 100.0% |

**Figure 1.8: The Incidence of Poverty by Household Composition**

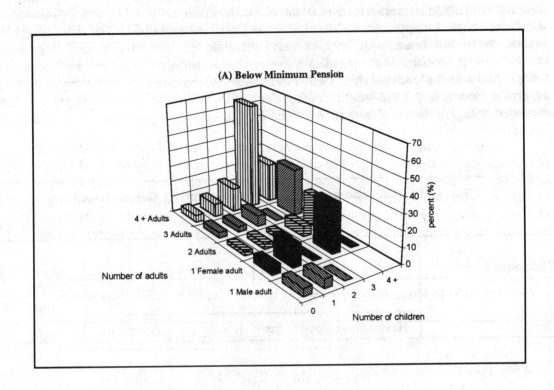

(A) Below Minimum Pension

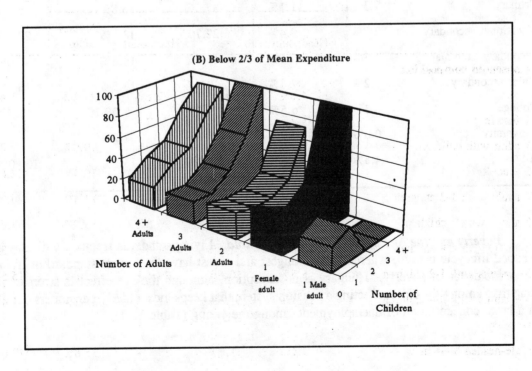

(B) Below 2/3 of Mean Expenditure

*Poverty and Education*. A strong inverse relationship exists between poverty and the education of the household head, working primarily through the labor market. (Table 1.10). Secondary or higher education virtually guarantees a level of living above the minimum pension, and college and university education puts all but 5 percent of people above the higher poverty line (2/3 of mean expenditures). In contrast, household heads with only primary education or less have a very high incidence of poverty—almost one-third of the population live in such households. This reflects a high incidence of unemployment among household heads with little education, or a casual relationship with the labor market and erratic income from employment. Although not shown in these data, a strong ethnic dimension is associated with low levels of education in Hungary, a relationship that is being perpetuated across generations.

### Table 1.10: The Incidence of Poverty and the Poverty Gap by Education of the Household Head

| Educational level | Below minimum pension | | Below 2/3 of mean expenditures | | Share of each category in total population |
|---|---|---|---|---|---|
| | Headcount | Poverty gap | Headcount | Poverty gap | |
| Less than primary | 13.1% | 14.5% | 51.0% | 20.7% | 9.9% |
| Primary | 7.3% | 11.1% | 37.3% | 16.8% | 26.6% |
| Vocational secondary | 2.9% | 9.4% | 22.7% | 13.7% | 28.6% |
| Secondary grammar | 1.3% | 15.6% | 15.1% | 14.4% | 7.0% |
| Other secondary | 1.2% | 7.5% | 12.3% | 13.5% | 16.2% |
| College | 0.3% | 6.5% | 5.5% | 8.0% | 6.5% |
| University | 0.0% | 0.0% | 5.1% | 7.7% | 5.2% |
| All | 4.5% | 11.7% | 25.3% | 16.2% | 100.0% |

*Poverty and the Age of the Head of Household*. Living standards frequently display an inverse U-shaped lifecycle pattern, whereby the youngest and oldest have the lowest standard of living and the highest incidence of poverty. Hungary is no exception, although the age effect is stronger among the young than among the old—reflecting a pension system that keeps most elderly pensioners out of poverty, and a large concentration of unemployment among the young (Table 1.11).

**Table 1.11: The Incidence of Poverty and the Poverty Gap by Age of Household Head**

| Age (years) | Below minimum pension | | Below 2/3 of mean expenditures | | Share of each category in total population |
|---|---|---|---|---|---|
| | Headcount | Poverty gap | Headcount | Poverty gap | |
| < 25 | 11.2% | 10.6% | 41.7% | 17.4% | 4.0% |
| 25-34 | 4.2% | 8.7% | 27.4% | 14.1% | 21.7% |
| 35-49 | 3.9% | 12.4% | 21.0% | 15.9% | 42.6% |
| 50-59 | 3.9% | 12.5% | 18.5% | 17.4% | 14.4% |
| >= 60 | 5.2% | 13.4% | 35.2% | 17.9% | 17.3% |
| All | 4.5% | 11.7% | 25.3% | 16.2% | 100.0% |

*Targeting Poverty Alleviation Efforts: Education and Employment Status are the Key Determinants of Poverty.* The analysis has indicated a bivariate relationship between poverty and several socioeconomic and demographic characteristics of households in Hungary. But what is the relative importance of each determinant of poverty, and what is its direct and indirect effects? For example, a low educational level is associated with low income and a higher probability of being poor, but in turn, it also increases the probability of becoming unemployed, which again exacerbates the probability of being poor. These determinants and their direct and indirect relationships are at the heart of an effective allocation of resources for alleviating poverty. This section reports the results of a basic multivariate analysis that captures the effect of all poverty correlates discussed so far. Two different models are used. The first one considers the full distribution of household expenditures and shows the contribution of each household characteristics to living standards (OLS estimation). The second model shows how each household characteristic affects the probability of being poor (probit estimation).

According to the OLS estimates, education makes the largest contribution to raising living standards, (Table 1.12). Households whose head has a college or university education have additional monthly household expenditures of HUF 5,560 and HUF 7,230, respectively—over households whose head has only a secondary vocational education (holding all other household characteristics constant). Socioeconomic category is the next most important determinant. It is noteworthy that, all else equal, being a pensioner lowers living standards among heads of households by more than does being unemployed. But if additional household members are unemployed and the household does not receive unemployment benefits, such a household has in fact the lowest living standard of any group. As expected, the composition of the household also matters, but less so than do the other variables. The coefficients of the age variables indicate that living standards peak at age 48.

The two poverty status models confirm that education and employment status are the key determinants of poverty. Temporary employees and those with less than primary education are clearly at greater risk of being poor than are other types of households. Households where the head is unemployed face a 5 percent greater probability of being poor (below the minimum pension) - and this almost doubles if they receive no unemployment benefits. All other things being equal, pensioners are not more likely than other groups to have a living standard below the minimum pension, but they are 12 percent more likely to fall below two thirds of the mean.

The models also confirm that larger households are more likely to be poor, but they show that after controlling for other socioeconomic characteristics, there is little difference between the effect of additional children and that of additional adults in the household. Female headed households are more likely to be poor, even if they have otherwise the same characteristics as male-headed households.

Finally, the results show that the probability to be poor is determined entirely by the economic and demographic characteristics of the household and is not additionally affected by the type of locality where one lives (Budapest, town or village). The fact that poverty is higher in towns and villages is due to the fact that more unemployed and low-educated people live there, and that demographic characteristics associated with poverty are more prevalent there.

| Table 1.12: Key Determinants of Poverty | | | |
|---|---|---|---|
| | Monthly household expenditures per adult equivalent (OLS estimation) | Poverty status (percentage points change in the probability to be poor) | |
| | | Below minimum pension | Below 2/3 of mean expenditures |
| Reference base[a] | 14,409* | - | - |
| Town | -307 | 0.08 | -0.52 |
| Villages | 172 | 0.46 | -1.48 |
| Temporary employee | -4,134* | 8.64* | 28.02* |
| Self-employed/sole proprietor | 2,982* | -0.25 | 2.28 |
| Unemployed (household head) | -2,662* | 4.99* | 18.99* |
| Pensioner | -3,022* | 0.45 | 12.27* |
| Other socioeconomic groups | -1,356* | 4.08* | 11.36* |
| Number of unemployed in household | -1,259* | 0.64* | 8.30* |
| No unemployment benefits | -1,021* | 3.97* | 8.41* |
| Number of adults in household | -1,172* | 0.50* | 4.28* |
| Number of children in household | -1,054* | 0.48* | 5.07* |
| Age of head | 246* | 0.01 | -0.06* |
| Age of head squared | -2.53* | | |
| Female headed household | -1,312* | 0.79* | 5.89* |
| Less than primary school | -2,029* | 3.97* | 18.59* |
| Primary or special post primary school | -1,438* | 1.91* | 11.48* |
| Secondary school | 2,648* | -0.33. | -8.09* |
| College | 5,560* | -1.17* | -14.14* |
| University | 7,228* | -2.24 | -12.37 |
| R² | 0.20 | - | - |

[a] The reference category is a household in Budapest, with a male head who is a permanent employee with secondary vocational education; * indicates significant difference from zero at the 90% confidence level.

## CHAPTER 2: THE CASH TRANSFER SYSTEM DURING TRANSITION

**Introduction**

Hungary has an extensive, generous array of cash transfer programs, consisting of three broad categories of benefits: contribution-based social insurance; income supplement "entitlements"; and household "means"-tested social assistance benefits. (Box 2.1 provides details on the programs offered under each of these categories). Much of the system is a carryover from the former regime's paternalistic package of cradle-to-grave benefits, whose financing was predicated on compressed wages and extensive labor-force participation. The majority of the benefit programs have in fact remained in tact throughout the transition[1] although inflation has eroded the value of some. Entire new "western" benefit packages (such as unemployment insurance and expanded categories of social assistance) have been overlaid onto this base; they are meant to help cushion households against the stress and strain of Hungary's economic transition, particularly the enormous job losses and widening income gap associated with an emerging market-oriented economy. Early in the transition, many people also sought to "cash in" on existing benefit packages from disability pensions, early retirement pensions, and child-leave programs as an alternative to open unemployment or simply as a way to meet daily living standards. As a result, in 1993 a full 40 percent of the population were receiving benefit subsidies or income supplements from Hungary's social program system, and were no longer engaged in gainful, full-time employment.

The full ramifications of this generous, pervasive system of benefit programs for both households and the economy can be seen in the numbers (Table 2.1). For example, across all households, cash transfers now account for almost one-third of disposable income; perhaps more revealing, a mere 9 percent of all households do *not* contain a recipient. A full 7 million or more Hungarians are eligible for benefits. And the cost of these cash transfers to the country is enormous. As a share of GDP, cash transfers rose from an already high figure of 14.6 percent in 1989 to 20 percent in 1993 and 19 percent in 1994. This level of spending is matched only by the most redistributive OECD economies, such as Sweden, the Netherlands, and France.

---

[1]  The government's austerity package of March 12, 1995, the 1995 budget, and the 1996 budget have, however, begun to dismantle and reconstruct some of these transfers. These changes are discussed later in this chapter, and in chapter three.

| Box 2.1:  Cash Transfer Programs, 1993 | | | |
|---|---|---|---|
| **Benefit** | **Eligibility** | **Amount and Duration of Benefits** | **Financing Source** |
| <td colspan="4">Social Insurance:  Benefits available largely as wage-based contributions by employee/employer, and used for income and employment contingencies.</td> | | | |
| 1.  Old age pension (entitlement) | Women who reach age 55 and men age 60, who have a minimum of 15 years of contributions (the minimum. pension) or 20 years of contributions (full pension). Some professions are allowed an early retirement after 10 years of service. | Earnings-based formula that takes account for years of service (=contributions) and variable proportion of earnings since January 1988. Legally set minimum pension is HUF 6,400 monthly. | Pensions Fund, from employer and employee payroll contributions. |
| 2.  Survivors pension | Surviving spouses and orphans. | Usually paid at half the deceased's old-age pension, but with the old-age pension minimum. | As above. |
| 3.  Disability pension | Loss of 67% of ability to work and no improvement expected within one year; must have specified number of years of service, and any subsequent earnings must be at least 20% less than prior to disability. | Same as for old-age pension. Eligibility can cease if disability is cured and/or if earnings reach level prior to disability. Same minimum as for the old age-pension. | As above. |
| 4.  Unemployment insurance | Loss of job, other than voluntary quit. One year of employment for minimum benefit; 4 years for full benefit. | In 1992, up to 18 months: 70% of last wage for the first 12 months, and 50% for remaining 6 months. The lower benefit threshold is the minimum wage; the higher threshold is 2 times the minimum wage. Since 1993, up to 12 months: 75% of last wage for the first 4 months; 60% for the remaining 8 months. The higher the benefit threshold for this second period is 1.75 times the minimum wage. | Solidarity Fund, financed primarily by payroll contributions from employers and employees but with some central budget support. |
| 5.  Pregnancy/ confinement allowance (THGY) | New mothers with at least one full year of social security contributions. | 100% of previous gross wage for 168 days, commencing 28 days prior to expected birth. Average payment is HUF 14,500 monthly. | Health Insurance Fund (HIF) from contributions. |

| | Box 2.1: Cash Transfer Programs, 1993 (cont.) | | |
|---|---|---|---|
| **Benefit** | **Eligibility** | **Amount and Duration of Benefit** | **Financing Source** |
| 6. Child care fee (GYED) | Women with at least one full year of social security contributions who choose to stay at home. | 65-75% of previous gross wage until child's second birthday. (Fathers eligible after child's first birthday.) | Central budget |

Entitlements: Benefits available as wage-income supplements for all citizens regardless of income or contributions to benefit schemes.

| | | | |
|---|---|---|---|
| 7. Child care allowance (GYES) | All mothers on part-time or full-time leave from work. Includes students. | Fixed amount, usually the same as the minimum pension (HUF 6,000 monthly). Paid until the child's 3rd birthday (10 years if the child is disabled). | Central budget |
| 8. Family allowance | Paid for all children until their 16th birthday (age 20 if in full-time education), including unborn children from 13th week of pregnancy. | For 2 parent families monthly payments of HUF 2750, 6500 and 11,250 for 1,2 and 3+children respectively. Equivalent amounts for one parent families - HUF 3250, 7500 and 11,850. | Central Budget |

Social assistance: benefits available as cash subsidies for people in "need" based either on a household means test or on characteristics closely correlated with poverty.

| | | | |
|---|---|---|---|
| 9. Third child allowance (GYET) | Either parent who stays at home with child. Income-tested to a maximum of 3 times the minimum pension per capita. | Minimum pension until the youngest child's 8th birthday. | Central budget, but paid through local authorities. |
| 10. Social assistance for the long-term unemployed | Registered with unemployment agency and providing evidence of job seeking, and no longer eligible for unemployment benefits. | Up to 80% of minimum pension based on a means test, until unemployment status ceases. Maximum payment is HUF 5,120 monthly. | 50% from central budget, and 50% from local governments; paid through local authorities. |
| 11. Various social assistance programs | Subsidy programs determined by local authorities. Different programs have different categorical eligibility rules, but all based on tests of income and poverty characteristics. | Variable, depending on program and assessment of local authority. | Local governments |

Note: This study focuses on six components of the cash transfer system: old-age and disability pensions, unemployment insurance, the family allowance, the child care fee (GYED), the child care allowance (GYES), and (various cash) social assistance programs as one group.

| | Insurance-Based | | | Entitlement | | Needs-based | |
|---|---|---|---|---|---|---|---|
| | Pension (all types) | Unemployment Insurance | Child Care Fee (GYED) | Family Allowance | Child Care Allowance (GYES) | Social Assistance Programs | Total |
| Number of persons eligible for benefits (thousands) | 2,600 | 410 | 143 | 2,276 children | 115 | 1,400[a/] 100 | 6,944 |
| Percentage of households receiving | 55.2% | 16.2% | 4.6% | 44.3% | 7.2% | 23.1% | 91.1% |
| Average monthly payment per individual (HUF) | 12,060 | 9,560 | 10,060 | 2,750[b/] 6,500 11,250 | 6,000 | 1,500[a/] 5,120 | 4,863 |
| Ratio to average net wage (of HUF19,215) | 62.8% | 49.8% | 52.4% | 14.3-58.5% | 31.2% | 7.8%[/a] 26.6% | 25.3% |

**Table 2.1: Major Cash Transfer Programs, 1993: The Numbers**

*Source*: Social Security Funds; National Labor Center; Ministry of Welfare.
[a/] The top figure is for discretionary social assistance; the bottom is for mandated social assistance for the long-term unemployed.
[b/] The top figure is for one child and two parents; the middle for two children and two parents; and the bottom for three children and two parents.

Hungary's extensive and generous package yields a range of recipients of social insurance, entitlement, and social assistance benefits. But who are they and, more importantly, do they include Hungary's poor? Are these programs benefiting those targeted by them, and what is the cost of trying to reach these target groups? What efforts has the government made to make the cash transfer system more target-efficient and cost-effective? And should some of the programs be restructured to make them more effective for Hungary's poverty groups? These questions are addressed in the remainder of this chapter.

**The Distribution of Cash Transfers: Do They Reach the Poor?**

Strictly speaking, only social assistance programs are conceived as antipoverty programs with payments being made on the basis of need. Of all the benefits, public pensions have the least poverty alleviation objective, although social redistribution is one of their three functions. (The other two being mandatory savings and insurance pensions for old age or disability.) Pensions are included in this analysis because they play a very important role in maintaining household income.[2] As mentioned, 91 percent of all households in Hungary receive some type of cash transfer (including pensions), for an average amount of HUF 13,520 monthly per household (table 2.2)—or 70 percent of the average net wage. The amount provides more that 30 percent of their disposable household income. Among the poorest 25 percent of households (those below two-thirds mean expenditure), 96 percent receive a social

---

[2]    In recognition of the multi-purpose objectives of public pensions, the analysis that follows is both inclusive and exclusive of pension incomes.

transfer, accounting for 50 percent of disposable household income. This comprehensive coverage of cash social transfers and at such high (relative) values is exceptional even among formerly socialist economies. But how are benefits distributed among all households, and is this distribution capturing the poor effectively?

| | | | | | | | | Transfers |
|---|---|---|---|---|---|---|---|---|
| **Table 2.2: Distribution of Cash Transfers by Socio-Economic Characteristics** | | | | | | | | |
| Percent of Households Receiving: | | | | | | | | |
| | Pension | Unemployment Benefit | Child care fee (GYED) | Family allowance | Child care allowance (GYES) | Social assistance (cash) | Any social transfer | Transfers other than Pension |
| **Income-earning status of household head** | | | | | | | | |
| Permanent employee | 27.3 | 16.8 | 6.3 | 64.0 | 9.6 | 22.8 | 85.5 | 72.8 |
| Temporary employee | 27.5 | 24.4 | 5.9 | 61.4 | 3.2 | 50.6 | 95.9 | 81.0 |
| Self-employed | 24.2 | 15.2 | 5.2 | 70.3 | 12.2 | 17.4 | 84.5 | 73.7 |
| Sole proprietor | 22.8 | 8.3 | 5.9 | 65.4 | 7.9 | 25.9 | 81.9 | 76.1 |
| Unemployed | 26.4 | 90.3 | 12.0 | 66.5 | 18.2 | 38.3 | 97.7 | 17.5 |
| Pensioner | 99.9 | 5.0 | 0.2 | 5.7 | 0.6 | 20.9 | 100.0 | 26.4 |
| Recipient of child care benefits | 23.7 | 28.3 | 40.1 | 100.0 | 63.0 | 47.6 | 100.0 | 100.0 |
| Other | 45.0 | 32.6 | 6.3 | 41.5 | 8.5 | 28.5 | 86.8 | 69.3 |
| **Household composition** | | | | | | | | |
| 1 male adult | 53.1 | 10.0 | - | - | - | 11.4 | 65.7 | 21.0 |
| 1 female adult | 88.2 | 1.3 | - | - | - | 20.0 | 90.4 | 20.9 |
| 1 adult with children | 13.5 | 11.9 | 3.4 | 96.4 | 11.6 | 44.7 | 98.4 | 97.1 |
| 2+ adults | 67.8 | 15.9 | 0.4 | 19.4 | 0.2 | 17.5 | 87.1 | 41.3 |
| 2 adults with 1-2 children | 8.8 | 22.7 | 14.4 | 98.9 | 22.0 | 27.5 | 99.9 | 99.2 |
| 2 adults with 3 children | 8.7 | 19.3 | 24.6 | 100.0 | 39.3 | 52.4 | 100.0 | 100.0 |
| 2 adults with 4+ children | 7.5 | 31.5 | 21.1 | 100.0 | 46.7 | 68.1 | 100.0 | 100.0 |
| 3+ adults with 1-2 children | 39.4 | 26.9 | 7.1 | 99.4 | 11.0 | 33.7 | 99.8 | 99.8 |
| 3+ adults with 3+ children | 52.9 | 39.4 | 15.1 | 100.0 | 35.6 | 74.0 | 100.0 | 100.0 |
| **Region** | | | | | | | | |
| Budapest | 51.2 | 8.1 | 1.9 | 38.0 | 6.6 | 16.0 | 86.7 | 47.3 |
| Towns | 48.7 | 15.7 | 5.4 | 47.5 | 6.6 | 22.5 | 90.8 | 60.3 |
| Villages | 56.8 | 21.4 | 5.4 | 44.4 | 8.4 | 27.9 | 94.1 | 62.4 |
| **All households** | 52.2 | 16.2 | 4.6 | 44.3 | 7.2 | 23.1 | 91.1 | 58.3 |
| Average monthly amount of transfer received by recipient households (HUF)[a] | 14,994 | 6,648 | 7,176 | 5,580 | 3,524 | 1,517 | 13,520 | 7,704 |

a/ Since the Household Budget Survey provided the data for this table these amounts are annual household figures divided by 12. (Because the HBS covers a 12-month period, the information on cash transfers is an aggregate of that period.) While some transfers (pension, GYED, GYES, and family allowance) are likely to be paid on a regular basis for an entire year, other transfers (unemployment benefits and social assistance) are not necessarily paid for an entire year. Thus, monthly totals derived by a simple division by 12 are imprecise. Annual amounts can be seen in Annex table A3.6.

*Distribution of Benefits Overall.* Pensions are the most widely received transfer, benefiting 52 percent of all households (Table 2.2). Although all households headed by a pensioner of course receive pensions, so, too do about one-fourth of all other groups in the income-earning status category. The households headed by non pensioners may receive pensions because one household member may be disabled or retired while the head continues to be active in the labor market. Among one-person female households, 88 percent of them receive a pension. As noted in chapter 1, this household group has a higher than average incidence of poverty—which is explained not only by the exclusive contribution of pensions in their income, but also by their relatively low amount. At HUF 10,550 monthly, the average pension of single women is 14 percent lower than the pension received by single male adults. (Annex Table A3.6) Moreover, these averages conceal large variation in pension amounts. Older pensioners who received their starting pension some years ago typically receive less then "new" pensioners.

The family allowance is the second most widely received social transfer, benefitting 44 percent of households according to the HBS. Households with children receive virtually universal coverage—99 percent or 100 percent in all but one category of households. The exception is a household comprising one adult with children, 4 percent of which do not receive the allowance. (The reason for this is not apparent.)

The child care fee (GYED) is paid to mothers who take a leave of employment to care for children at home. Almost 5 percent of households receive this fee. The child care allowance (GYES) is paid to mothers on part-time or full-time leave from work who are not eligible for GYED or who choose a third year of child care leave. About 7 percent of households receive this allowance. It is concentrated among permanent employees, the self-employed, and the unemployed (and, by definition, "recipients of child care benefits").

About 16 percent of households receive unemployment insurance benefits, as do 90 percent of those whose head is unemployed. Almost 30 percent of households whose main source of income is child care benefits also receive unemployment benefits. Temporary employees are also beneficiaries of this program. Unemployment insurance beneficiaries are concentrated in households with more than two adults and/or more than three children, suggesting an unhappy coincidence of large household size and fragile links with the labor market—both of which are strong determinants of poverty. More households in villages receive unemployment benefits (21 percent of households) than do households in towns (16 percent) or in Budapest (8 percent), clearly reflecting regional labor-market variations. However, the average amount of the benefit is higher in Budapest than elsewhere, probably reflecting higher wages in Budapest than elsewhere in the country.

About 23 percent of all households receive benefits from social assistance programs, but which provide the smallest cash transfer of all benefit programs—HUF 1,517 monthly per recipient household. The distribution of social assistance over all households shows some distinct concentrations:

- *Region*: 85 percent of recipients live in towns or villages; the regional concentration is strongest in the North.

- *Household composition:* 18 percent of recipients are single adult households (with or without children), despite the fact that these households comprise only 8 percent of the population. Large households also capture a disproportionate share of benefits.

- *Gender of head of household:* one-third of social assistance beneficiaries are female-headed households (23 percent of all households).

- *Education:* social assistance recipients are found among all education groups, roughly in proportion to their share of the population. But households whose head has less than a primary education are overrepresented, and those whose head has a college or university education are under-represented.

- *Socioeconomic status:* more than one-half of social assistance recipients are households headed by a permanent employee (such households comprise two-thirds of all households, but their incidence of poverty among them is quite low); pensioner and temporary employee households are the most overrepresented among social assistance recipients.

- *Unemployment:* 22 percent of social assistance beneficiaries are households that contain an unemployed person (17 percent of all households). (Box 2.2 discusses the special relationship between unemployment and social assistance).

---

### Box 2.2: Unemployment and Social Assistance

The relationship between unemployment and social assistance is particularly important, both because poverty is concentrated in households that contain unemployed members and because many households exhaust their unemployment insurance benefits and require special social assistance to fill the gap. Roughly one-third of households that contain an unemployed person receives social assistance, and the ratio is higher when the household exhausts its unemployment benefits. The program also reaches more households headed by an unemployed person (see table); almost two-thirds of poor households headed by a person whose unemployment benefits have run out receive social assistance. But when the unemployed person is not the head of household member, less than one-half of poor households receive social assistance.

| Unemployment and Social Assistance | | |
|---|---|---|
| | Percent of households receiving social assistance % | Percent of poor households receiving social assistance: |
| | | Below minimum pension % | Below 2/3 of mean expenditure % |
| Unemployed head with unemployment benefits | 37.0 | 43.4 | 45.1 |
| Unemployed head without unemployment benefits | 50.9 | 63.2 | 63.9 |
| Other unemployed household member with unemployment benefits | 26.3 | 41.1 | 35.8 |
| Other unemployed household member without unemployment benefits | 34.2 | 49.1 | 40.6 |
| All | 31.0 | 46.0 | 40.6 |

*Distribution of Benefits by Poverty Line*.  About 60 percent of households below the minimum pension poverty line receive a pension (Table 2.3).  The figure rises to 65 percent among households between the minimum pension and two-thirds of mean expenditure, and declines thereafter (figure 2.1). Poor households receive an average of HUF 11,321 monthly (table 2.3), well above the minimum pension of HUF 6,400—but because the amount is contributing to the expenditure of the entire household, it is not sufficient to raise each recipient household above the poverty line on a per adult equivalent basis. In contrast, the average monthly pension received by a household above the subsistence minimum is HUF 16,693 monthly (figure 2.2).  Thus, a greater percentage of poor households receive pensions, but the amount they receive is lower (which of course partly explains their poverty).  The concentration coefficient[3] of pensions at the household (not individual) level is -0.06 indicating that pension transfers are redistributive in favor the poor.

| Table 2.3:  Distribution of Cash Transfers by Poverty Level | | | | | | | | |
|---|---|---|---|---|---|---|---|---|
| Percent of households receiving: | | | | | | | | |
| | Pension | Unemploy-ment insurance | Child care fee (GYED) | Family allowance | Child care allowance (GYES) | Social assistance | Any social transfer | Transfers other than pension |
| Below minimum pension | 59.9 | 27.0 | 3.9 | 48.4 | 11.0 | 39.0 | 96.9 | 68.4 |
| Between minimum pension and 2/3 of mean household exp. | 64.5 | 21.3 | 3.9 | 39.6 | 7.5 | 27.6 | 96.2 | 58.5 |
| Between 2/3 of mean household exp. and subsistence minimum | 57.0 | 16.0 | 4.8 | 43.0 | 7.7 | 23.8 | 94.6 | 57.3 |
| Above subsistence minimum | 41.4 | 12.7 | 4.9 | 47.3 | 6.3 | 18.7 | 85.2 | 57.9 |
| All households | 52.2 | 16.2 | 4.6 | 44.3 | 7.2 | 23.1 | 91.1 | 58.3 |
| Monthly amount received by recipient households: | | | | | | | | |
| Below minimum pension | 11,321 | 6,874 | 6,814 | 5,668 | 4,070 | 2,212 | 13,379 | 9,036 |
| Between minimum pension and 2/3 of mean household exp. | 13,505 | 6,542 | 5,168 | 5,705 | 3,554 | 1,631 | 13,815 | 7,825 |
| Between 2/3 of mean household exp. and subsistence minimum | 14,997 | 6,720 | 6,218 | 5,677 | 3,408 | 1,448 | 13,709 | 7,724 |
| Above subsistence minimum | 16,693 | 6,619 | 8,763 | 5,447 | 3,529 | 1,362 | 13,196 | 7,473 |
| All households | 14,994 | 6,648 | 7,426 | 5,588 | 3,524 | 1,517 | 13,520 | 7,704 |

---

[3]  The *concentration coefficient* determines how effective a transfer is at reaching the poor.  It shows the concentration (cumulative percentage) of one variable (say, pensions) when recipients are ranked by income (or expenditure). The concentration coefficient ranges from -1.0 (all transfers are received by the poorest recipient) through 0 (all recipients receive the same amount of transfer) to +1.0 (all transfers are received by the wealthiest recipients). From a poverty perspective, a transfer is "very good" if the concentration coefficient is strongly negative, showing that the poor receive most of the transfer. It is still "good" if the concentration coefficient is less than the gini coefficient - that is, it still improves income distribution.

Unemployment insurance benefits are more strongly targeted at the poor: 27 percent of the poorest households receive them, compared with only 13 percent of households above the subsistence minimum. The average monthly benefit does not vary much by expenditure level of the recipient, because the benefit formula has a strong tendency to the minimum, creating in essence a flat-rate payment. As such, unemployment benefits make a strong contribution to equalizing the distribution of living standards (as reflected by a concentration coefficient of -0.11).

The family allowance is a universal benefit, payable for all children up to a certain age regardless of the parents' income standing. According to this study, neither the incidence of its receipt nor its average monthly amount varies by the expenditure level of the recipient household. For example, the proportion of recipient households below the minimum pension is identical to the proportion of recipient households above the subsistence minimum, and the amount they receive is virtually identical. This relatively flat distribution (as measured by a concentration coefficient of +0.04) indicates that the family allowance is not a particularly well targeted antipoverty program. This finding differs from previous findings that the family allowance is progressive and well-targeted. (See, for example, Jarvis and Micklewright 1992; and van de Walle et al. 1994).[4] Yet a similar analysis carried out by TARKI with three years of panel data (1992-1994) and using the same weighting system for children, yields findings similar to this study (TARKI 1994 and 1995).

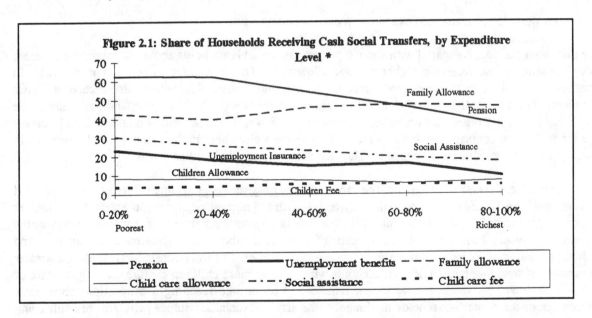

Figure 2.1: Share of Households Receiving Cash Social Transfers, by Expenditure Level *

* Persons quintiles of household expenditure per equivalent adult

The incidence patterns of the child care allowance and the child care fee differ markedly. Although both are paid to mothers who are on leave from employment, the allowance is a fixed amount, while the fee is a proportion of previous wages. As such the child care allowance is a progressive cash transfer; the child care fee is strongly regressive. The allowance reaches 11 percent of households below

---

[4] One of the principal reasons for the differing findings is the choice of equivalency scale. This study uses the OECD equivalency scale (see Box 1.1) which accords a weight of 0.5 to children. Previous work has used a per capita basis, which accords a weight of 1.0 to children (likewise to all adults). When households are ranked on the basis of either per capita expenditure (income) or per equivalent adult expenditure (income), two rather different patterns emerge: the former is inclined to place large households at the poorest end of the distribution, the latter does not. Given the close correlation between household size and number of children, the per capita ranking places more children and, by definition, more family allowance receipt at the lower end of the distribution. This in turn shows a more progressive, better targeted family allowance.

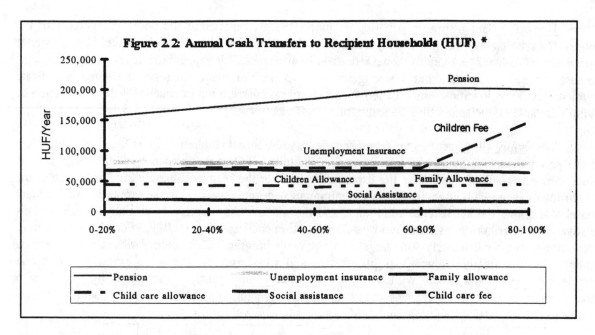

Figure 2.2: Annual Cash Transfers to Recipient Households (HUF) *

* Persons quintiles of household expenditure per equivalent adult.

the minimum pension, compared with about 6 percent among all households above the minimum pension; poor households also receive a higher average allowance. The concentration coefficient is -0.05. In contrast, the child care fee goes predominantly to wealthier households, which also receive a higher payment. The concentration coefficient for the child care fee is +0.22. The regional distribution of the child care fee clearly reflects labormarket circumstances. Fewer than 2 percent of households in Budapest are fee recipients, compared with 5.4 percent of households elsewhere in the country; but households in Budapest receive an almost three times higher fee than households in other towns.

Of all cash transfer programs, the range of <u>social assistance programs</u> offered by various local governments are targeted at the poor most directly—with the highest negative concentration coefficient of any social transfer (-0.16). Social assistance reaches some 39 percent of households below the minimum pension, compared with 19 percent of households above the subsistence minimum. And although small in absolute amounts, the social assistance benefits of the poorest households are greater than those of wealthier households. Households with three or more children capture the largest share of benefits, followed by single female parent families. Yet, despite reaching a proportionately greater percentage of the poorer households in Hungary, the array of social assistance programs are still being targeted inefficiently, excluding some needy recipients, while leaking benefits to other less needy socioeconomic groups. For example, 61 percent of households whose expenditures are less than the minimum pension are not receiving any social assistance, while 19 percent of households above the minimum subsistence receive at least some cash transfer, including large amounts by sole proprietor households. The pattern of exclusion and leakage is not random, but is partly correlated with certain household and regional characteristics. While an in-depth analysis of this issue is ongoing,[5] preliminary results suggest that households in Budapest, households with permanent employees and pensioners, smaller households, and households with more educated members are less likely than others to receive social assistance when they are poor. On the negative side, leakage towards nonpoor recipients is more extensive in villages, in households headed by a temporary employee or unemployed person, and in both large and female-headed households. Some of these targeting errors are due inevitably to using those same characteristics (unemployment, and number of children) as eligibility criteria since they tend to be

---

[5] Among other documents, see "Social Welfare Services of the Local Authorities," Working document no. 1 of the Hungary Central Statistical Office, August 1994.

correlated with poverty; of course they are not in each case. But some of the errors also stem simply from the administrative inadequacies of social assistance programs. As discussed in the next chapter, social assistance leakage requires greater vigilance by analysts and policy makers.

*Is the Overall Distribution Pro-Poor?* The average amount of all social transfers received by households varies remarkably little by household expenditures (Figure 2.2, Table 2.3 and Annex Table A3.6). This is true both with and without pension incomes. The concentration coefficient of all transfers is -0.02, indicating in essence a fully egalitarian distribution —not particularly good from a poverty perspective. Yet, overall transfers to the poorest households represent a much greater percentage of their income and cover a much greater percentage of their expenditure than among wealthier households— and around four times greater share of household expenditure (table 2.4).[6] (The table also shows that social assistance and unemployment benefits are the most pro-poor transfers, while again the child care fee is the least pro-poor.) As such the cash transfer system is progressive, contributing proportionately more to the well-being of the poor than to the nonpoor. In the absence of cash transfers, income and expenditures inequalities would be exacerbated.

**Table 2.4: Poor to Non-Poor Cash Transfer Ratios**
**(Shares Captured by Households Below the Minimum Pension)**

|  | Pension | Unemploy benefit | Child care fee | Family allowance | Child care allowance | Social assistance | All Social Transfers | Non-pension transfers |
|---|---|---|---|---|---|---|---|---|
| Recipients of social transfers | 1.44 | 2.13 | 0.80 | 1.02 | 1.75 | 2.09 | 1.14 | 1.18 |
| Amounts received per recipient household | 0.67 | 1.04 | 0.78 | 1.04 | 1.15 | 1.62 | 1.01 | 1.21 |
| Amounts received per all households | 0.98 | 2.21 | 0.62 | 1.07 | 1.99 | 3.38 | 1.15 | 1.43 |
| Share of household expenditures | 3.63 | 6.65 | 2.29 | 3.31 | 7.50 | 11.17 | 3.95 | 4.74 |

Note: Ratios are for households below the minimum pension relative to households above the subsistence minimum.

## Cost Efficiency: How Much Is Coming to the Poor?[7]

While the preceding results indicate that Hungary's cash transfer system has reasonably been successful at reaching the poor (that is external efficiency), they do not indicate the cost at which its success is achieved—that is, how much of the money being spent on transfers is reaching poor households. A comprehensive analysis of the cost effectiveness of the transfer system is outside the scope of this study, but partial measures of targeting efficiency are available along two dimensions: the average amount of transfers that go to one poor person (Table 2.5), and the average number of poor persons helped per HUF 1 million of transfers spent (Table 2.6). These calculations provide only partial

---

[6]   Because the equivalent ratio for income is 2.4:1, cash transfers are still progressive regardless of whether household income or expenditure are used to measure the living standard of households.

[7]   This section is based on the premise that all cash transfers have a legitimate role in moderating poverty. As noted above - paragraph 2.4 - it is acknowledged that poverty alleviation is often not the single, nor indeed the prime objective of some cash transfers programs.

measures of cost efficiency because information on administrative costs is unavailable, which should in principle be added to the amount of transfers to compare different parts of the system.

The first column of Table 2.5 shows the total amount of a given transfer divided by the total number of people in the country who were poor before receiving the transfer (the "pretransfer" poor). This broad measure of the cost of reaching one eligible poor person captures transfers that go to nonpoor or program leakage. The second column shows the average amount of a transfer actually received by the pretransfer poor; it excludes the cost of leakage from the numerator, and the denominator consists of pretransfer poor recipients only (as opposed to all pretransfer poor). Ideally, under perfect targeting, leakage would be zero, and both columns would be identical. In practice, poverty-oriented programs should be larger in the second column that the first column, indicating that the cost of cash transfers is more efficient when targeted at poor beneficiaries than at the potential target group as a whole. But as shown clearly in the table, none of the cash transfers meets this condition when the minimum pension is the poverty line; in contrast all transfers but the family allowance meet this condition when the higher poverty line is used. All else equal, targeting is more likely to be successful when the higher poverty line is used.

| Table 2.5: Monthly Transfers to One Pretransfer Poor Person - (Average HUF) | | | | |
|---|---|---|---|---|
| | Below minimum pension | | Below 2/3 of mean expenditure | |
| | Average transfer paid per poor person | Average transfer received by poor person | Average transfer paid per poor person | Average transfer received by poor person |
| Pension | 10,540 | 8,465 | 6,293 | 7,421 |
| Unemployment benefit | 4,685 | 2,640 | 1,319 | 2,112 |
| Child Care Fee | 2,386 | 1,873 | 455 | 1,593 |
| Family allowance | 8,564 | 1,811 | 2,551 | 1,566 |
| Child care allowance | 1,735 | 874 | 345 | 882 |
| Social assistance | 2,266 | 1,005 | 474 | 677 |
| All social transfers | 11,078 | 7,137 | 7,483 | 5,968 |

An alternative measure for examining the cost of reaching the poor is the number of poor persons helped per HUF spent on social transfers—that is, the poverty impact of different transfer programs after normalizing for the size of the program (or for how much it spends). Table 2.6 shows three progressively narrower measures: the number of pretransfer poor per 1 million HUF spent on a given transfer program, or the size of the potential target group; the number of pretransfer poor actually reached by a given transfer per HUF1 million spent; and the number of poor persons lifted above the poverty line as a result.

| Table 2.6: Number of Pretransfer Poor Persons Helped per HUF 1 Million of Transfers (Poverty Line of 2/3 of Mean Expenditures) | | | |
|---|---|---|---|
| | Average number of poor people | Average number of poor recipients | Average number of poor recipients lifted out of poverty |
| Pension | 13.2 | 9.6 | 5.8 |
| Unemployment benefit | 63.2 | 25.3 | 8.7 |
| Child care fee | 183.1 | 18.1 | 6.9 |
| Family allowance | 32.7 | 23.5 | 8.9 |
| Child care allowance | 241.3 | 41.2 | 11.7 |
| Social assistance | 175.8 | 66.7 | 8.6 |
| | | | |
| All social transfers | 11.1 | 11.0 | 6.4 |

Social assistance reaches the most poor people per HUF 1 million spent—an average of 66.7 poor recipients. The child care allowance reaches 41 poor people per HUF 1 million spent; all other programs reach 25 or fewer poor people. As expected, the pension system reaches the fewest number of poor people at the highest cost per poor person, because it transfers the greatest amounts and is not oriented at poverty alleviation. Per HUF 1 million spent, the child care allowance (GYES) is the most "cost" efficient at lifting people out of poverty, despite the fact that the program is not oriented specifically towards alleviating poverty. Three programs (unemployment benefits, the family allowance, and social assistance) are equally cost efficient at lifting poor people out of poverty—about 9 persons per HUF 1 million spent. The pervasiveness—and success—of Hungary's transfer system is highlighted by the fact that it spends HUF 1 million per 11.1 pretransfer poor people in the country—reaching, in one way or another, 11 of those people, and lifting an average of 6.4 of them out of poverty.

***Closing the Poverty Gap: What Percentage of the Poor are Lifted Out of Poverty?*** Because *pensions* are by far the largest cash transfer, it is not surprising that they make the greatest contribution to keeping people out of poverty—62 percent of households that receive pensions are lifted above two-thirds of mean expenditure.(Table 2.7) This finding for pensions is normal since pension is the main source of income for most recipients especially those having little or no earned income. Because pensions are based on previous wages, their effect on poverty comes from the pension calculation method and its subsequent indexing (and people's place in the prepension wage distribution), and not from any intended poverty targeting (although the latter can be an objective of minimum pension policy).

The second most effective program is the child care fee (GYED), which lifts 43 percent of its recipients above the poverty line. The effectiveness of the GYED might at first seem surprising, given that the program is the most regressive cash transfer in the system. But because the child care fee is a wage-replacement benefit and is thus quite high, absence of it can and does often make the difference between being poor and not. The effect is particularly strong in Budapest, which as was indicated earlier, has the highest child care fee. The abolition of this program may have some poverty implications unless the recipients are able to return to work, despite the fact that only a relatively small percentage of households currently receive the fee (4.6 percent). The simulations in the next section will make this point clearer.

## Table 2.7: The Impact of Social Transfers on Alleviating Poverty

Percent of Pretransfer Poor Households Who are Lifted Above 2/3 of Mean Expenditure by the Social Transfer

| | Pen-sion | Unemploy ment Insurance | Child care fee (GYED) | Family allowance | Child care allowance (GYES) | Social assistance | All Social trans fers | Non-pension transfers |
|---|---|---|---|---|---|---|---|---|
| **Regions** | | | | | | | | |
| Budapest | 68.9 | 36.2 | 78.6 | 34.7 | 43.5 | 16.6 | 65.9 | 41.5 |
| Towns | 62.7 | 41.3 | 37.5 | 43.1 | 29.0 | 17.2 | 61.6 | 47.8 |
| Villages | 58.3 | 38.0 | 40.4 | 37.0 | 24.2 | 11.0 | 57.2 | 42.5 |
| **Household composition** | | | | | | | | |
| 1 male adult | 64.3 | 52.6 | - | - | - | 0.0 | 61.5 | 31.1 |
| 1 female adult | 59.8 | 81.4 | - | - | - | 14.4 | 60.0 | 19.5 |
| 1 adult with children | 33.7 | 73.0 | 50.1 | 52.7 | 26.9 | 23.8 | 57.2 | 57.2 |
| 2+ adults | 66.3 | 44.0 | 47.2 | 36.7 | - | 15.5 | 65.8 | 39.9 |
| 2 adults with 1-2 children | 47.6 | 40.8 | 51.1 | 41.2 | 35.3 | 19.2 | 55.8 | 53.5 |
| 2 adults with 3 children | 11.5 | 14.5 | 36.9 | 49.1 | 30.3 | 3.2 | 57.0 | 56.5 |
| 2 adults with 4+ children | 0.0 | 0.0 | 0.0 | 20.9 | 21.3 | 10.1 | 24.8 | 24.8 |
| 3+ adults with 1-2 children | 46.4 | 24.2 | 34.4 | 35.7 | 21.1 | 11.6 | 51.8 | 42.8 |
| 3+ adults with 3+ children | 20.3 | 7.0 | 0.0 | 17.8 | 5.7 | 3.2 | 27.4 | 24.3 |
| **Income earning status of household head** | | | | | | | | |
| Permanent | 66.9 | 43.9 | 50.0 | 44.3 | 40.1 | 17.7 | 62.1 | 53.3 |
| Temporary employee | 21.2 | 22.1 | 0.0 | 27.7 | 100.0 | 15.7 | 40.0 | 42.0 |
| Self-employed | 47.3 | 29.6 | 38.7 | 29.5 | 13.3 | 9.2 | 49.6 | 42.4 |
| Sole proprietor | 100.0 | 100.0 | 0.0 | 77.2 | 100.0 | 0.0 | 90.5 | 84.9 |
| Unemployed | 40.7 | 34.7 | 33.9 | 24.9 | 10.3 | 13.4 | 43.0 | 39.5 |
| Pensioner | 62.7 | 34.5 | 43.1 | 24.0 | 13.4 | 12.0 | 63.1 | 20.6 |
| Recipient of child care benefits | 13.7 | 27.8 | 20.1 | 38.2 | 9.5 | 0.0 | 44.6 | 42.8 |
| Other | 32.9 | 50.9 | 56.1 | 37.1 | 28.8 | 24.6 | 51.3 | 48.0 |
| All | 62.3 | 39.2 | 42.6 | 39.2 | 29.7 | 14.3 | 60.7 | 44.5 |

Both unemployment insurance benefits and the family allowance lift 39 percent of pretransfer poor recipients out of poverty. This figure is fairly uniform across different parts of the country, but it varies widely across types of households. (Table 2.7)

A high rate of poverty alleviation can be achieved more easily with a small target group. For example, the poverty alleviation effect is strongest among households with a single adult, a category that contains only a small percentage of beneficiaries. At an extreme are sole proprietors, a category for which pension, GYES and unemployment insurance all lift 100 percent of recipients out of poverty. Yet because only 8 percent of sole proprietor households receive unemployment benefits and they are not a very poor group, any transfer has a greater likelihood of lifting beneficiaries above the poverty line. In contrast, a low poverty alleviation targeting can be due soley to poor targeting, but also to good targeting combined with transfer amounts that are too low, especially for high poverty groups. This point is illustrated by the effect of the unemployment benefit on temporary employee households— although they have a high incidence of unemployment insurance receipt, they are one of the poorest groups, so the benefit leaves many of them in poverty. The family allowance received by households with many children has a similar effect: for households consisting of 2 adults and 3 children (for whom coverage is 100 percent), the allowance lifts 49 percent of pretransfer poor above the poverty line. This figure drops to 21 percent of households with 4 or more children, reflecting an insufficient benefit amount that keeps poverty high among this group.

The figures in table 2.7 for social assistance are particularly interesting. Although social assistance is the most progressively distributed transfer, it has the lowest poverty alleviation effect—much of which is due to low benefit amounts per recipient household (HUF 1,517 monthly/on average). The poverty alleviation role of social assistance must be strengthened considerably, both by increasing financial resources available to it (possibly from savings in other parts of the system) and by targeting it more effectively. Social assistance is currently most effective for single-parent households, 45 percent of which receive assistance and almost one-fourth are lifted out of poverty. The incidence of receipt is also high among households with 3 or more children and the long term unemployed, but for them social assistance merely bridges part of the poverty gap.

***Improved Living Standards: Transfers Received as a Proportion of Poverty Gap.*** Even when they do not lift households above the poverty line, cash transfers can have a major impact on households' living standards (Table 2.8). As shown earlier, the poverty gap averages 16 percent of the relative poverty line of two-thirds of mean expenditures. The total amount of cash transfers received by the poor below this poverty line is three times larger than the poverty gap. Thus, without the transfers, the poverty gap would be almost four times larger. The last line of Table 2.8 also shows how transfers to the nonpoor (those above the subsistence minimum) compare with the poverty gap: they are almost four times larger than the post-transfer poverty gap, and larger than transfers to the poor. Even after excluding pensions, transfers to the nonpoor are still larger than the poverty gap. In fact, by themselves, the family allowances to the nonpoor would almost be sufficient to cover the entire poverty gap. It is clear that the family allowances should be reformed.

## Table 2.8: Social Transfers and the Poverty Gap

| | Pension | Unemployment benefit | Child care fee | Family allowance | Child care allowance | Social assistance | All social transfers | Non Pension transfers |
|---|---|---|---|---|---|---|---|---|
| | Social Transfers to Households below 2/3 of Mean Expenditures as Percentage of Poverty Gap | | | | | | | |
| **Region** | | | | | | | | |
| Budapest | 230.2 | 28.5 | 1.1 | 40.8 | 4.4 | 15.0 | 320.1 | 89.8 |
| Towns | 189.9 | 32.1 | 4.8 | 56.0 | 7.0 | 11.8 | 301.5 | 111.7 |
| Villages | 162.6 | 32.9 | 5.5 | 50.1 | 6.7 | 9.7 | 267.5 | 104.9 |
| **Household Composition** | | | | | | | | |
| 1 male adult | 366.7 | 39.9 | - | - | - | 16.7 | 423.2 | 56.5 |
| 1 female adult | 463.0 | 2.2 | - | - | - | 7.8 | 472.9 | 10.0 |
| 1 adult with children | 43.9 | 7.2 | 2.5 | 99.6 | 13.5 | 23.2 | 190.0 | 146.1 |
| 2+ adults | 305.1 | 34.4 | - | 15.1 | - | 9.2 | 363.8 | 58.7 |
| 2 adults with 1-2 children | 23.6 | 44.1 | 12.4 | 79.2 | 17.6 | 7.0 | 183.9 | 160.3 |
| 2 adults with 3 children | 15.9 | 38.1 | 13.6 | 156.7 | 18.3 | 27.3 | 269.9 | 254.0 |
| 2 adults with 4+ children | 2.5 | 19.7 | 13.9 | 168.4 | 18.1 | 24.4 | 246.9 | 244.4 |
| 3+ adults with 1-2 children | 67.2 | 35.1 | 3.9 | 67.9 | 6.4 | 9.2 | 189.7 | 122.5 |
| 3+ adults with 3+ children | 35.1 | 18.8 | 9.9 | 83.0 | 6.5 | 28.0 | 181.3 | 146.2 |
| **Income-earning status of household head** | | | | | | | | |
| Permanent employee | 63.9 | 30.9 | 5.3 | 72.5 | 9.0 | 9.5 | 191.0 | 127.1 |
| Temporary employee | 55.3 | 8.5 | 0.9 | 47.2 | - | 19.7 | 131.6 | 76.3 |
| Self-employed | 105.3 | 21.7 | 2.1 | 60.7 | 13.5 | 10.7 | 214.1 | 109.8 |
| Sole proprietor | - | - | 62.9 | 66.4 | - | 2.6 | 131.9 | 131.9 |
| Unemployed | 28.1 | 79.0 | 9.0 | 67.7 | 9.9 | 16.0 | 209.7 | 181.6 |
| Pensioner | 424.5 | 14.4 | 0.5 | 14.5 | 0.8 | 10.2 | 465.0 | 40.5 |
| Recipient of child care benefits | 20.4 | 39.1 | 29.6 | 92.4 | 21.4 | 7.8 | 210.7 | 190.3 |
| Other | 133.2 | 53.1 | 3.6 | 45.7 | 4.6 | 23.7 | 263.9 | 130.7 |
| **All** | 182.8 | 32.0 | 4.6 | 50.9 | 6.4 | 11.2 | 287.9 | 105.1 |
| **Social transfers received by households above subsistence minimum as percentage of the poverty gap** | | | | | | | | |
| All | 247.4 | 30.1 | 15.5 | 92.2 | 8.0 | 9.1 | 402.3 | 154.9 |

**How Should the Cash Transfer System Be Restructured?**

At present, about 7 million people are eligible for one or another of the cash transfers, and 91 percent of households benefit from them. This level of coverage is quite remarkable by any standard. At the same time, the aggregate incidence and value of transfers is very uniform across the income (expenditure) distribution. This was also the situation in the past, when wages were compressed and labor force participation was high—and little has since been done to reform the programs whereby they reflect the growing inequalities in market incomes. Despite their wide coverage, cash transfer amounts are insufficient to lift the neediest persons out of poverty. Although the *majority* of social transfer recipients are no longer poor after receiving the transfers, about 27 percent of households that receive social transfers still remain below two-thirds of mean expenditures. Clearly, in these cases, the amount of the transfer is insufficient to close the poverty gap. Put another way, too many people in Hungary are benefitting from too many cash transfers, and amounts are insufficient to prevent those who have little or no alternative income from slipping into poverty. Why is this, and why are the cash social transfers proving ineffective at preventing growing poverty? One of the reasons is that the country has gone through a major recession, reducing incomes across the board. That cash transfer incomes have maintained their real value much more so than have labor incomes has played a critical role in preventing even more people from falling into poverty. This is one of the major conclusions from the analysis in this chapter. But the analysis also shows clearly that if cash transfers were organized in a different way, their poverty alleviation impact could be much stronger.

First, some well-identified groups of the population are poor simply because they are falling through the cracks of the cash transfer system. One such group consists of households with long-term unemployed members especially the household head, for whom insurance-based unemployment benefits have run out, and no alternative (major) source of regular income has been substituted.[8] Another such group consists of female recipients of the child care allowance (GYES), for whom the (although small) amount is a very critical source of income. The expiration (or planned abandonment) of this program (discussed later) runs the risk of creating a small group of very poor households who may have no other alternative but social assistance. Last, a pocket of poverty appears to exist among elderly single-women pensioner households, for whom additional (social) assistance may be necessary. These points are discussed further in chapter 3.

In the same way that cash transfer programs are missing some people, they are catching others who could do without them. Even among programs with a more explicit anti-poverty focus— social assistance and (to a lesser extent) the family allowance—benefit "leakage" to the non-poor is substantial. Almost one-third of the money transferred through these programs goes to households above the subsistence minimum. For social assistance, 24 percent of payments go to such households. (Table A3.12) Somewhat ironically, the cash transfer programs that are not explicitly anti-poverty programs—pensions, unemployment insurance, and the child care fee—are more effective at lifting people above the poverty line, given their broad coverage (pensions), their value (the child care fee), and their targeting (unemployment benefit).

---

[8]  Such households are theoretically eligible for means-tested social assistance for the long-term unemployment. Either they are not receiving this benefit or the benefit amount is so small (just more than HUF 5,000 month) that it is insufficient to lift these households out of the most severe poverty.

***Reform Measures of March 1995.*** In March 1995, the government of Hungary announced several proposals to modify some elements of the cash social transfers system as part of a broader austerity package. These proposals are significant because, for the first time, they challenge the principle of universal entitlement, recognize the different ability of individuals and households to benefit from the emerging market economy, and begin to shift welfare responsibility from the state to individuals. The main innovation in the proposals is the introduction of means testing for the family allowance and child care benefits. Certain modifications have been made since the announcement of the proposals. As this report was being prepared, details of the changes, likely to be introduced in April 1996, are as follows:

- An income cap is to be applied to the family allowance. Eligibility for the full amount is to be based on net income of less than HUF 18,000 per capita monthly, in the previous calendar year. Eligibility for partial amount is to be based on an income of HUF 18,001 to 19,500; income above HUF 19,500 would make a household ineligible for benefits.[9]

- Households with 3 or more children are to be eligible for family allowance regardless of their income. Households with permanently ill or disabled children are treated in this same way.

- The child care allowance (GYES) and the child care fee (GYED) are to be merged; the new provision should not last longer than two years and should be means tested, based on the same criteria for the family allowance.

Several additional modifications are also adopted in the 1996 budget—replacement of the pregnancy allowance, the introduction of a new income-supplement allowance, greater emphasis on social assistance, and a two-year time limit on the social assistance receipt by the long-term unemployed (as well as changes in various aspects of the eligibility rules for unemployment benefit).

***How Will the Reforms Perform? The Results of Simulations.*** For the purpose of this report, the impact of the new family allowance and child care benefit measures on the incidence of poverty among different types of households has been simulated. By way of comparison and illustration, simulations of the effects of alternative targeting rules based on the observed correlates of poverty have been applied -in particular, the number of children in the household, the number of unemployed in the household, and the educational level of the head of household.

Because the government proposals were announced in 1995 (and modified in early 1996) but the HBS data used in this report pertain to 1993, the new lowest income threshold for the family allowance was adjusted to reflect price changes.[10] The HBS data available for this work also consisted only of household records, excluding such individual data as the age of children. This shortcoming required some approximations to simulate the effect of changes in the age caps for the family allowance, and the

---

[9] In the case of a single parent the monthly per capita ceiling is HUF 23,400.

[10] Given the nature of Household Budget Survey data, the simulations have been made with gross income figures rather than net.

pretransfer inclusion of families with three and more children.[11] For these reasons, more attention should be given to orders of magnitude in the numbers than to precise estimates.

The simulation results (Table 2.9 and Annex Table A3.9) suggest that a combination of means targeting for the family allowance, increasing amounts paid to families with three and more children, and a greater role for social assistance could be very effective at reducing the poverty incidence among those groups in Hungary for whom it is currently highest. The government's current measures are an important first step in this direction, but there is still some way to go.

*Family allowance proposal 1*. Current government plans to restructure the family allowance would have the following impacts on the *incidence of poverty*:

- The overall effect would be slight, but poverty incidence would not decline;

- With the minimum pension as the poverty benchmark, the incidence would remain the same in the aggregate; with two-thirds of mean expenditures as the benchmark, it would rise from 25.3 percent to 26.1 percent.

- Among the very poor (those below the minimum pension), the effect would be strongest in households of 3 or more adults and 1 to 2 children, and in households of temporary employees (for whom the incidence of poverty wold rise from 19.3 percent to 22.1 percent).

Regarding their *fiscal impact*, the reforms would achieve gross savings of around 22 percent of current spending, roughly the same proportion as households eliminated from eligibility. Net savings, however, would be less, because the means-test will require administrative costs, and because benefits would leak to some families of more income than reported.

---

[11]    More sophisticated simulations based on individual data could be carried out at a later date.

| Table 2.9: Selected Cash Transfer Reforms: Effects on the Incidence of Poverty and Fiscal Viability | | | | | |
|---|---|---|---|---|---|
| | Poverty Line | | | | Fiscal difference |
| | Below minimum pension | | Below 2/3 of mean expenditure | | |
| | Poverty incidence | Difference in poverty incidence | Poverty incidence | Difference in poverty incidence | |
| Current situation | 4.5% | --- | 25.3% | --- | --- |
| Family allowance proposal 1 (FA1) | 4.6% | +0.1 | 26.1% | +0.8 | -22% |
| Family allowance proposal 2 (FA2) | 3.8% | -0.7 | 24.0% | -1.3 | -5% |
| Family allowance proposal 3 (FA3) | 4.3% | -0.2 | 25.6% | +0.3 | -18% |
| Family allowance proposal 4 (FA4) | 4.3% | -0.2 | 25.7% | +0.4 | -19% |
| Family allowance proposal 5 (FA5) | 3.5% | -1.0 | 23.6% | -1.7 | -2% |
| Child care proposal | 5.2% | +0.7 | 26.6% | +1.3 | -57% |
| Social assistance proposal | 3.6% | -0.9 | 24.7% | -0.6 | 0.0 |

Key:
FA1 = Current government plans
FA2 = Higher monthly payments for 3+ children.
FA3 = Higher monthly payments for 2+ unemployed.
FA4 = Higher monthly payments for poorly educated household head.
FA5 = FA2 + FA3 + FA4
Child care proposal = current government plans
Social assistance proposal = reallocation of funds to households under poverty lines

The poverty profile in chapter 1 identified pockets of poverty, one of which is among households with 3 or more children. The government's plan to leave these households with an automatic entitlement to the family allowance is a positive step. However, evidence from this chapter indicates that the amount of transfers to families with 3 and more children is insufficient to lift them out of poverty. The value of the family allowance has not been increased since 1993, and has been eroded by inflation that has been running in the 20 to 30 percent annually range. In the absence of any increase in the nominal value of the family allowance in 1996, its real value will decline even further, with grave consequences for these families. The social assistance program could be used to compensate the neediest families for this difference, but because the program has several major weaknesses, its ability to reach the neediest families effectively must be questioned. As such, using the family allowance system to give families with three or more children larger benefit amounts could be more effective. The Hungarian government has taken the first major step in this regard by leaving these families outside the scope of means testing and keeping them in the program. The next major step would be to increase the value of the family allowance to families with three and more children. Its poverty alleviation effect would be significant.

*Family allowance proposal 2.* The potential gains from targeting higher monthly family allowance payments at families with three and more children are shown with additional simulations. The key assumption is that the family allowance is increased by HUF 3,750 monthly per child (the amount corresponds to the current amount received for the third child in two-parent households). Simulation results show that, in practice, such large increases may not be necessary, but it is useful to show the upper limit of what can be achieved with indicator-based targeting using easily observable socio-economic characteristics and the family allowance as the tool. Targeting by the number of children would significantly reduce the overall incidence of poverty (by 0.7 percentage points relative to the minimum pension poverty line, and by 1.3 percentage points relative to the higher poverty line). Of course, different types of households would be affected differently. Poverty in large households would disappear entirely, indicating that such targeting can be effective at alleviating poverty, but also indicating that the amounts in this simulation are too generous. (Further simulations could define amounts that, for example, would reduce the incidence of poverty in households with three or more children to the level found in households with one to two children.) Since a fairly strong positive correlation exists between the number of children in a household and the number of unemployed, the FA2 scenario would also reduce poverty in households headed by an unemployed person. Another target group—households whose head has less than a primary education—would also benefit although to a lesser degree.

*Family allowance proposals 3, 4, and 5.* Three other simulations have been done for comparative purposes. The poverty profile reveals two other deep pockets of poverty: households that contain two or more unemployed members, including the household head, and households whose head has less than a primary education. These characteristics could also be targets for larger family allowance payments to families that contain children. The FA3 and FA4 simulations demonstrate the impact of targeting these characteristics on poverty. FA5 shows the impact of increasing the allowance if *either* one of the three conditions (three or more children, two or more unemployed adults, and head with less than primary education) is met.

Targeting by unemployment and low educational level is virtually poverty-neutral in the aggregate. That is, it does not have a significant poverty reduction effect. However, particular groups would enjoy some positive effects. Targeting by the number of unemployed (FA3) would have the strongest effect in the largest households— those with three or more adults— since unemployment is concentrated in these families. Targeting by educational level (FA4) would also help these households, as well as those with two adults and many children, and of course those whose head has less than a primary education. Targeting by education would also be the only approach that would reduce poverty significantly among the temporary employees.

These results suggest that much can be achieved by combining the different criteria (FA5), since doing so would reach all desired target groups, and would remain within the current family allowance budget (Indeed, there is room for some savings). As stated earlier, the optimal amounts would have to be determined, and the simulations in Table 2.9 must certainly be seen as an upper limit of what can be achieved. The results suggest that poverty can be reduced significantly with indicator-based targeting using the family allowance as the instrument. Of course, if social assistance targeting could be improved or a general income supplement applied effectively, these options might be more cost-effective instruments for reaching households in which unemployment or low education is the main cause of poverty.

*Child care allowance and fee.* According to the simulations, the elimination of the child care allowance and fee and the institution of the new child care benefit would increase poverty from 4.5 percent to 5.2 percent below the minimum pension, and from 25.3 percent to 26.6 percent below the relative poverty line (Table 2.9 and Annex Table A3.10). But the new benefit scheme would yield substantial fiscal savings, at 57 percent of the budget. The most adverse impact would be on households that contain many children, those headed by an unemployed person, and by definition, those dependent on child care benefits. For example, in households with two adults and four or more children, the incidence of poverty would increase from 19 percent to 27 percent; in households with three or more adults and three or more children, the incidence of poverty would almost double to 40 percent. (These figures do not include the impact of the family allowance changes, which in part will be mitigating.) Thus, this part of the reform program runs the risk of hurting some poor groups unless they can re-enter the labor market or qualify alternatively for unemployment benefits or social assistance. Given the extent of fiscal savings implied by the reform, it should be possible to increase the amount of the new benefit and/or improve its targeting and still achieve significant savings.

As an alternative, and indeed implied in the austerity package, *social assistance* could play a greater role in poverty alleviation efforts. It is currently the most progressively distributed transfer and, after unemployment insurance benefits, the most effectively targeted transfer at the poor. But is suffers from three serious problems: its benefits are being leaked to the nonpoor; it misses some needy households altogether; and the transfer amounts are inadequate for meeting the needs of many poor recipient households. These problems require urgent attention. Notwithstanding the difficulty of targeting social assistance more effectively with means tests or more precise indicator-based targeting, eliminating, say, leakages of social assistance benefits to households above the government's new family allowance income cap would create a fund that could be reoriented towards the neediest recipients. The amounts saved under this scenario would constitute 36 percent of social assistance now received by those below two-thirds of mean household expenditures, and 136 percent of social assistance now received by households below the minimum pension. Allocating these funds proportionately to current recipients would reduce poverty by, respectively, 0.9 and 0.6 percentage points (Table 2.9). Doing so would especially benefit one-parent households, very large households, households with unemployed heads, households dependent on child care benefits, and households with less educated heads.

## CHAPTER 3: CONCLUSIONS AND POLICY RECOMMENDATIONS

This chapter draws on the analysis in the preceding two chapters to provide some directions for policymakers to improve upon their poverty alleviation efforts as Hungary proceeds on its course of economic transition. The thrust of the chapter is to provide recommendations about how the cash transfer system can be restructured to play a more effective role in poverty alleviation. Of particular concern are the specific groups of the poor who are falling through the social safety net. The recommendations herein are mindful of the budgetary implications of a system overhaul, and thus advocate changes in poverty alleviation interventions that are amenable to current resource constraints.

Although an important element and especially critical for some groups of the population, restructuring the cash transfers system should be conceived of as part of a more extensive poverty alleviation strategy. Broad based economic growth—generating more jobs and higher wages, as well as providing the government with the revenues needed to finance social transfers—is of uppermost importance. Here, too, restructuring cash transfers can play a role. By reducing aggregate expenditure, and addressing the distorted incentive system, a restructured cash transfer system could both promote economic growth and be more efficient and effective in poverty alleviation.

### Analysis of the Incidence of Poverty and the Poverty Gap

To recapitulate briefly, the analysis in chapter 1 showed the following:

● *The incidence of poverty has increased in the period 1989-93.* The magnitude of the increase is sensitive to the poverty line chosen and to assumptions about income underreporting in household surveys. The increase in the incidence of poverty is a function primarily of declining real household incomes; because household income is densely concentrated around the positioning of the poverty line, even a small decline in income levels can lead to substantial increases in the incidence of poverty. A growing income inequality, which in reality is the product of an unequal distribution of the decline in national income, has also played a part in the rising incidence of poverty. The income decline has been most severe for the poorest 10 percent of the population, whose real household expenditure fell by more than a third during the period; conversely, the wealthiest income group has actually gained in real terms. The result is a significant increase in the share of the population below the minimum pension, from 1.6 percent of the population to 8.6 percent.[1]

● *Poverty is concentrated close to the poverty line.* Poverty in Hungary is largely "shallow". That is, the average income (or expenditure) of those below the poverty line is not substantially less than the poverty line. The *poverty gap*—the average shortfall of household income (expenditure) as a percentage of the poverty line—ranged from 15 to 20 percent from the late 1980s to 1993. But, importantly, the increase in the incidence of poverty has not been associated with any increase in the poverty gap; if anything, the poverty gap has narrowed slightly. This

---

[1]    The real value of the minimum pension declined from 1989 to 1993. The share of the population under the 1993 minimum pension is thus less.

trend is not surprising, as more people whose incomes are close to the poverty line fall just below the line.

- *Some deep pockets of poverty exist.* Hungary contains some households (individuals) whose income falls far short of even the lowest poverty line; they are considered the very poorest.

*Who Are the Poor in Hungary?* An examination of the characteristics of poverty groups in Hungary yields the following profile:

- Among socioeconomic groups, the deepest poverty is among households whose head is *unemployed, temporarily employed, or dependent on child care benefits as the main source of income*. About one-fifth of such households live below the minimum pension.

- Poverty among *pensioners* is slightly above average. Very elderly female pensioners living ᵢ one, however, are among the very poorest.

- In households affected by unemployment, poverty is deeper if the *head of household is unemployed* than if another member of the household is unemployed. *If the head is unemployed and does not receive unemployment insurance benefits, then incidence of poverty is very high:* more than 40 percent of such households are below the minimum pension.

- The regional variation in the incidence of poverty is not very pronounced. Moreover, *regional differences in incidence of poverty can be explained entirely by differences in the socioeconomic and demographic composition of the population.*

- Demographic characteristics are important indicators of poverty. The incidence of poverty is lowest in nuclear households with one or two children. It rises steadily with the number of children and is *especially deep in households with two adults and four and more children, and in households with 3 adults and 3 and more children.* Among these households, one in five lives below the minimum pension The corollary to these findings is that poverty among children is somewhat more pervasive than among the population at large.

- *Poor children live primarily in villages, and in households whose head is poorly educated and does not have more than a temporary attachment to the labor market.* This finding is worrisome since it indicates the likelihood of inter-generational poverty.

- Hungary displays the normal inverse U-shaped lifecycle pattern of poverty, but *the age effect is stronger among the young than the old*, reflecting the relative well-being of pensioners and the high unemployment rate among the young.

- There is a distinct gender dimension to poverty. *Poverty is deeper among female-headed households*, especially if they are single adults with children.

- A strong inverse relationship exists between poverty and the education of the household head. Secondary or higher education virtually guarantees a level of living above the minimum pension, and college and university puts all but 5 percent of the population above the higher poverty line of two-thirds of mean expenditure. *Almost one-third of the population live in households whose head has a primary education or less; among these households, around 40 percent fall below two-thirds of mean expenditure.*

- The incidence of poverty among the Roma population is almost six times as high as among the non-Roma population. This ethnic group is associated with most of the key correlates of poverty: long-term unemployment, large family size, and poor education level.

*Shifts between Transient and Permanent Poverty.* Some of the population groups in poverty in 1993 were already experiencing poverty prior to the transition. Through the 1980s, poverty was already affecting poorly educated and low-skilled individuals who had limited labor market opportunities as well as large families, the very elderly, and the gypsies. The recession and the structural changes associated with the economic transition have exacerbated their financial situation. New groups have also been lowered into poverty—the unemployed (especially the long-term unemployed who have exhausted their unemployment insurance benefits), mothers (particularly single mothers) on extended child care leave, and persons earning a living from casual employment. The extent to which any of these groups is likely to remain in poverty in the longer run is unclear. There appears to be a great deal of movement by households in and out of various relative income/expenditure positions. Between 1993 and 1994, almost 40 percent of households changed their relative position by two or more deciles. However, those in the lowest income decile—the poorest—have moved far less, and their characteristics are rather predictable: poor education, young or very old, unemployed over the long-term and gypsies. Some 300,000 people are estimated to be in permanent poverty in the period 1992-1995. (TARKI, 1995)

*Poverty and the Labor Market.* What has determined the winners and losers from the transition thus far? The most important determinant is labor-market status. Income from employment, self-employment, and business (but primarily wage income) are the main contributions to individual and household income (Figure 3.1). Labor income is a function of a job-holding, age, education and work skills, and location. Aggregate labor incomes declined by almost as much as the decline in GDP during 1989-93, but the decline was much more a function of job losses than of real wage declines. As such, those who kept a regular job fared reasonably well, particularly in so far as formal-sector jobs provide access to a second job as an other important source of income. Highly educated employees in private sector companies, often associated with foreign investment, have seen substantial real wage gains. In contrast, less educated and semi-skilled workers and public-sector employees have fared less well and experienced real wage declines. Of sources of household income, employment incomes (wages) were already the most unequal, and their dispersion across the income groups increased markedly in the transition years. Earnings inequality in Hungary is now on par with that of Western Europe (Rutkowski 1995).[2]

---

[2] The average earnings of the top quintile of Hungarian workers is now 3.7 times higher than the average earnings of the bottom quintile. This compares with ratios of 3.4 in the United Kingdom, 3.0 in France, 2.5 in Germany, and 2.1 in Italy (OECD 1993).

The reverse of regular employment and (near) constant real wage income is unemployment, casual work, extended child care on state support, or withdrawal from the labor force altogether (in many cases on disability pension arrangements). These are the real losers of the transition. Their access to regular wage income has essentially ceased. In some cases, where cash transfers are tied to previous wages (unemployment insurance benefits, disability or early retirement pension, and the child care fee) the situation is tolerable. But extreme poverty is emerging in other cases. The situation of the long-term unemployed is particularly dire. Former workers who have exhausted wage-related unemployment insurance benefits and who have not found regular reemployment are among the very poorest. The social safety net, including the purposely designed social assistance for the long-term unemployed, is apparently not working.

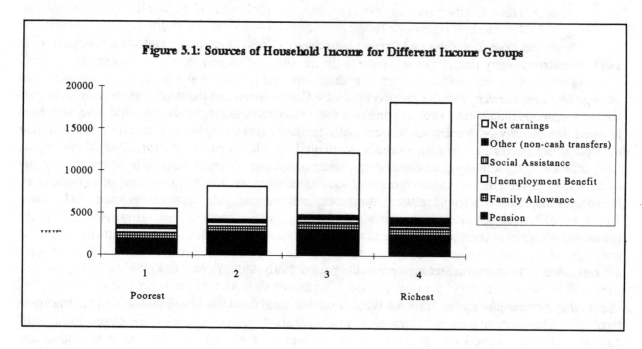

**Figure 3.1: Sources of Household Income for Different Income Groups**

## The Cash Transfer System

As detailed in chapter 2, Hungary offers a generous array of cash transfer programs. The transfer system includes contribution-based social insurance, income supplement entitlements, and means-tested social assistance. In 1993, cash transfers provided around 31 percent of net disposable household income, accounting for 20 percent of GDP. In that year, no fewer than 91 percent of Hungarian households were receiving one cash transfer or another; pensions alone were reaching 52 percent of households, and the family allowance was reaching 44 percent of households. In the past two years, public expenditure on cash transfers has fallen, but the number of recipients has remained largely unchanged. Benefit levels have therefore suffered. The analysis in chapter 2 indicated that:

- *Cash transfers have helped maintain disposable income.* As the share of labor income in aggregate disposable household income has declined in the transition years, cash social transfers which, in the aggregate, maintained their real value through 1993 have become more important.[3] In a static sense, cash transfers have prevented many households from falling into poverty. Indeed, cash transfers have lifted about 60 percent of households above the higher poverty line, two-thirds of mean household expenditure.

- *But cash transfers fail to prevent poverty.* Cash transfers are evenly distributed across income groups (Figure 3.1), just as they were in the past. The combined value of cash transfers is barely distinguishable whatever the household income level. Together, the wide distribution of cash transfers and their relative "blindness" to need (or household income level) means that some households—including transfer recipient households—are left in poverty because of low benefit amounts. More than one-quarter of households who receive social transfers remain below the higher poverty line.

- *Different cash transfers have played different roles during the transition.* Some have been more effective than others at preventing poverty. In general, social insurance-based transfers tied to previous wages and designed to replace wage income (pensions, unemployment insurance benefits and the child care fee) have been most effective at alleviating poverty even though this was not their specific aim. (These transfers alone account for 15 percent of GDP, however.) Social assistance has been least effective at alleviating poverty, due primarily to poor targeting and inadequate transfer amounts for those most in need.

## Household Coping Strategies

When faced with macroeconomic change, primarily through the labor market, individuals and households are not passive. They adopt various strategies to reduce vulnerability and to preserve their standard of living as best as they are able. Two features of coping behavior among Hungarians are particularly noteworthy:

- *Increased participation in the hidden (second) economy.* By definition, reliable data on this trend do not exist, but many signs point to substantial participation and significant earnings from grey and black-economy activities. This is true for all sorts of people—those with small businesses, the self-employed, formal-sector employees with second jobs, the registered unemployed, and pensioners.

- *Households transform and reconfigure themselves to maximize access to social transfers and minimize tax obligations.* The longitudinal study of a working-class neighborhood in Budapest offers many interesting insights into how households organize themselves to access more state benefits (Box 3.1).

---

[3] According to the HPS, this trend continued throughout 1994, when cash transfers accounted for 35 percent of household income.

| Box 3.1: Coping Strategies during Economic Transition: Evidence from a Working Class Neighborhood in Budapest, 1992 | | |
|---|---|---|
| **Level** | **Event** | **Coping Strategy** |
| Individual | Decline in public-sector industrial employment | Increased search for service-sector jobs. |
| | Increase in unemployment | Increased participation in second economy, both grey and black economies. |
| | Shift in state support for child care from workplace to home | Some mothers with young children remain at home to take advantage of state benefits (cash payments). |
| | Increase in public transport tariffs | Poor are more inclined to "free-ride" (ride without paying) as non-poor have greater access to subsidized fares due to more regular travel patterns. |
| Intra-household | Decline in employment and other market incomes | Households restructure to access more state benefits (e.g., pensioners living together but not marrying; young adults "adopting" grandparents to obtain access to the housing market, both privatization and renting). |
| | Rising food prices | Members extend their household to friends and relatives. |
| | Rising energy prices | Individuals operate small informal businesses from home (e.g., dressmaking, hairdressing, beautician). |
| | Rising costs of home maintenance | Households change in consumption patterns—less protein, cheaper varieties, etc. They grow own produce. |
| | | Households reduce consumption by turning off appliances; pensioners heat only one room. Bills often go unpaid for months. |
| | | Households reduce expenditure on (rented) house maintenance. Few poor households take opportunity to purchase public housing. |
| Inter-household | Need for short-term credit | Poor households take out ad hoc informal loans from neighbors and relatives. |
| | Rising costs of urban living | Poor families with young children, especially gypsy families, are inclined to send young children to live with grandparents in the countryside, or move back to the rural areas. |

*Source*: "Poverty and Vulnerability in Angyalfold, Hungary." Research project on Urban Poverty and Social Policy in the Context of Adjustment. Urban Development Division, World Bank, February 1995.

## Alleviating Poverty -- The Big Picture

There are two aspects to poverty in Hungary: the quite widespread shallow poverty, in one sense, a *relative* poverty phenomenon, (as noted by Ferge in the 1980s), and the small but deep pockets of poverty. Shallow poverty comprises people close to the higher poverty line of two-thirds of mean household expenditure; deep poverty comprises those who fall below the minimum pension poverty line. These patterns of poverty are not dissimilar from those in Western Europe and other Western countries. Yet the income distribution in Hungary is still much more equal than in neighboring Western countries, and the respective roles of market incomes and social incomes are still quite different. Addressing poverty starts by redressing this imbalance: at the aggregate, market incomes must rise, and social incomes must fall. The two are not unconnected.

The recent Country Economic Memorandum for Hungary[4] illustrates that growth is necessary for achieving fiscal stability and securing Hungary's welfare system in the future. But attaining a moderate growth rate first requires changes in the level and composition of public expenditure. As Hungary's cash transfer system absorbs a large share of public expenditure, its restructuring is unavoidable if resources for growth are to be released.[5] From the perspective of alleviating poverty, economic growth will be positive as it increases labor demand and supports productivity-based real wage increases (although some caveats apply as discussed in Box 3.2). The shallowness of much of Hungary's poverty suggests that economic growth would be a very effective cure, serving not only the unemployed and the low paid, but those on extended child care leave and those who have withdrawn from the labor force with minor disabilities.

But reaping these gains necessitates reducing the aggregate level of spending on cash transfers, and restructuring many programs. Using the following principles to reform cash transfers would serve well the interests of poverty alleviation:

- An adequate and effective social safety net, based strictly on need.

- A social insurance system that provides appropriate coverage for insurable life-cycle risks—old-age, sickness, disability, and child-bearing/rearing—but which avoids abuse (for example disability pensions), and which does not over-tax workers.

- A social security system that provides the right incentives for working, seeking higher-paying jobs, saving and paying taxes; any policy reform must avoid any further weighting of the incentive system away from formal-sector employment toward state benefits.

---

[4] Hungary: Structural Reforms for Sustainable Growth, 1995. A World Bank Country Study, Washington, D.C.

[5] The negative impact of the high spending on cash transfers on the economy goes beyond public expenditure and fiscal deficit: the high payroll taxes necessary for funding some of the transfers has a dampening effect on employment and can affect the competitiveness of firms, and high wage-replacement benefits can have a serious effect on incentives to work.

- A benefits system that supports measures to prevent people slipping into more permanent and deeper poverty.

- Recognition that individual and household behavior does not respond passively to change.

## Dealing with Shallow Poverty

The appropriate policy response to the phenomenon of shallow poverty is complicated, not least of which because people in this poverty category are a heterogeneous group; it includes some pensioners, low-paid employees, some of the unemployed, and some of the households with a large number of children. The appropriate policy response for each of these groups differs. Moreover, evidence suggests that the movement of people (households) in and out of shallow poverty is substantial.

---

**Box 3.2: Helping the Poor Return to Productive Employment**

For working age people, including those who have withdrawn from the labor force or who are only partially active, the most effective poverty reduction strategy would be the resumption of economic growth and the accompanying increase in labor demand. The appropriate policy framework for this is discussed in the recent Country Economic Memorandum (ibid). But the experience of OECD countries in recent years suggests that economic growth alone may not generate sufficient employment to return unemployment to very low levels, or if it does it may be at very low wage rates (the U.S. experience). Policies that make working more attractive and welfare dependence less attractive, and policies that make the unemployed more employable and potentially more productive, are increasingly considered to be important determinants of high levels of employment. Extracting in part from a recent OECD report (the Jobs Study), the following recommendations can be made for Hungary:

- Reduce non-wage labor costs to promote greater formal sector employment. In particular, lower the payroll taxes levied to meet pension, health, and unemployment obligations.
- Rearrange unemployment benefits to encourage the take-up of new jobs, including low-paid, part-time, and casual jobs. The approach that has ben used in various OECD countries is to continue paying cash transfers beyond unemployment to people who take up low-paid jobs, to ensure that they are better off in work than on welfare alone.
- Place more emphasis on up-grading and modernizing the educational levels and skills of the low-paid, the long-term unemployed, mothers on child care leave, and those with minor disabilities to enable them to become more productive workers. These categories of people should be given priority places in the Regional Training Centers.
- Modify the income tax system to provide incentives for people who shift the composition of their income away from social transfers to market incomes, either by taxing benefits and/or giving relief to new wage earners.

---

*Pensioners* are a particularly important population group in Hungary; after "permanent employees," they comprise the largest single group of households close to the higher poverty line. Among all households, 52 percent receive a pension income, and pensions provide more than 10 percent of GDP in the national budget and more than 25 percent of disposable household income. This report does not address pension system issues per se, which have already been discussed in the recent Country Economic Report; rather it focuses on the poverty perspective only. By focusing here on only one of the three objectives of public pension policy -- namely social redistribution -- the reader should not interpret the message of this report as differing from the Economic Report. On the contrary, the broader pro-growth message of this report implies reform of the public pension scheme. But in this section emphasis is necessarily on the first pillar of the pension system, and its role as a source of income for the elderly.

Cash transfers paid as pensions have both a significant absolute and a relative impact on poverty: they lift more than 60 percent of recipient households above two-thirds of mean expenditure and they are mildly redistributive at the household level. Of course, pensions could be made even more effective at combating poverty. One mechanism would be to raise the level of the state-provided minimum citizens' pension and ensure that it becomes a genuine minimum—that is no one entitled to a pension would receive less. This scheme could easily be affordable if the value of state-provided pensions received by top income pensioners were reduced. One group of pensioners that warrants special attention consists of elderly pensioners (often women) living alone, for whom the pension is their only source of income, and who (apparently) are receiving less than the minimum pension. This small group is in deep poverty; a modest increase in their pension would make a huge difference. Alternatively, they could receive an income supplement, paid as social assistance.

*Households with three or more children* are another population group that is over-represented in shallow poverty. This number of children is closely correlated with the low educational level and poor labor-market status of the household head. As such the number of children can also be used as proxy for other variables closely associated with poverty but which may be more difficult as a characteristic for targeting. Although not reported here, it is also known that children's educational attainment (as measured by years of schooling) is closely associated with the number of children in the household, as exemplified by the Gypsy community in particular.[6] This interaction between many children in the family, poor educational attainment, and poor labor-market status creates inter-generational poverty. As a poverty group, these households should be high on the priority list of Hungary's policymakers.

*The family allowance* is the main cash transfer program for preventing poverty among children; it has clearly made an important contribution to this goal in recent years. But previous research has shown that the family allowance can do even more, and many recommendations have been forwarded to improve its targeting. (The recommendations have focused on taxing the family allowance, targeting by categorical indicators, using means tests, and applying a combination of these.) This report confirms that the family allowance can play a much more critical role in alleviating poverty. Targeting the family allowance alone more effectively could virtually eliminate poverty below two-thirds of mean expenditure.

As discussed at length in chapter 2, measures announced by the government in March 1995 (and subsequently amended and adopted by Parliament) tackle universal entitlement to the family allowance for the first time and attempt to target the transfer to needier households with children. The instrument is a combination of means (income) tests and indicator-based targeting - the retention of the family allowance in all families with three and more children. The simulations at the end of chapter 2 clearly show the importance of this latter feature, although it should be noted that the income threshold per se

---

[6]    See Kertesi, G. et al: "The Education and Employment Situation of the Gypsy Community: Report of the 1993/94 National Sample Survey". ILO/Japan Project on Employment Policies for Transition in Hungary, Working Paper No. 17, Budapest, October 1994.

would not eliminate many households with three and more children (maybe 5 percent at most). These measures represent an important step forward, but three important problems remain. *First*, given the acute problems associated with means testing in Hungary (the data presented in this report bear witness to this problem), very few households would be excluded from an entitlement on the basis of income. As such budgetary savings would be scant; indeed, it is quite likely that the cost of administering the means tests will outweigh the financial gains from eliminating a few families. *Second*, inflation continues to erode the value of the family allowance, thereby mitigating its role as an anti-poverty instrument for the neediest households. The simulations in chapter 2 illustrate the powerful poverty alleviation impact of increasing the family allowance for those with three or more children, a group most frequently found in poverty. But to afford larger transfers for the neediest families will necessitate finding savings elsewhere. Eliminating eligibility in other selective well-off groups could do the rest.

The *third* problem is the so-called "welfare trap" (Box 3.3). The shift from a universal transfer to a means-tested transfer could act as a disincentive for people to improve their market incomes, since in doing so they might forfeit the family allowance and become worse off (or at least not better off). The sliding scale that determines the withdrawal of the allowance (HUF 18,000 to 19,500 per capita monthly) is designed in part to minimize the effect of the welfare trap. How successful it will be will emerge over time. Some modifications might be necessary.

---

**Box 3.3: The Welfare Trap**

As Hungary begins to dismantle its "universal" cash transfer programs, especially the family allowance, it faces another problem—the so-called "poverty trap," or the "welfare trap". The trap is caused by the payment of <u>means-tested</u> benefits—that is, only if the recipient can prove to have an income below a certain threshold (however defined). As the person becomes less needy, perhaps because he or she finds a job or receives a pay increase, the benefits are withdrawn, reducing the gain from working. Indeed, if benefits are taken away fast enough, all the extra income gained from working may be cancelled out. In this situation, welfare benefits become a large disincentive to finding a job, working more hours, or finding a higher-paying job.

Since this trap cannot be avoided entirely, the real question is how the harm it causes can be minimized. Here, too, there are no easy answers. Reforming the tax and benefit system is one option. The level of income at which benefits begin to be withdrawn can be raised or lowered, for instance, thus determining the depth of poverty among poor people when the trap is sprung. The rate at which benefits are withdrawn can be varied: a high rate would make the trap difficult to escape, but would apply to relatively few individuals a low rate would make escape easier, but would catch many more people. Evidence from around the world suggests that, on balance, a tougher trap that catches fewer people is best.

A variation on this theme addresses the disincentive to take up low-paid jobs and forego benefits—that is, paying more generous benefits to people in work, to ensure that they are much better off with jobs than without. In the United Kingdom a family credit is paid to families with children in which one person is working at least 16 hours a week. Low-paid Americans have been able to claim an earned income credit since 1975.

57

## Helping Those in Deep Poverty

Among the pockets of deep poverty, one group is particularly vulnerable—the long-term unemployed, who have exhausted their wage-related unemployment insurance benefits and have been unable to find a job. Long-term unemployment is found among prime-age workers (both male and female), the poorly educated, and the unskilled or semi-skilled; it also has a strong locational dimension (particularly, in the northeast). In theory, the long-term unemployed who are active job seekers are entitled to a means-tested social assistance program, introduced in 1993 for this particular target group. Yet the level of payment—up to 80 percent of the minimum pension—is a very modest amount, and quite insufficient to have any meaningful impact on severe poverty. This program needs urgent review. Among other reforms, the level of the transfers should be increased significantly (though not beyond the minimum wage), and wherever possible the payment should be combined with a job-search test, and—as appropriate—active reemployment programs.

*Long-term unemployment* is a problem facing many West European countries. It has been the subject of many experiments, many reports, and many conferences, including a workshop in Budapest.[7] There are no easy solutions to this problem; indeed, it has proved to be one of the most difficult challenges facing western countries in the past few years. Experience to-date suggests that programs for the long-term unemployed must be tailored specifically, locally adapted, and focused narrowly, reflecting the specific characteristics and needs of the clients and reflecting local labor-market circumstances. Tying a social payment to participation in a work-oriented program, not simply job search, seems to be critical to keeping the long-term unemployed active.

In addition to the long-term unemployed, those with a casual association with the labor-market, and those on leave from work to raise young children are also among the poorest. With regard to the latter, *GYED and GYES* are to be merged under the March 1995 austerity plan, and become contingent on means tests, whose income threshold would be similar to the family allowance. The simulations in chapter 2 suggest that doing so could have a negative impact on poverty, particularly among some socio-economic groups. This is not surprising, since a significant amount of income would be eliminated from recipient households, particularly those that receive wage-related GYED. The replacement allowance—if around the minimum pension, as discussed—would be considerably less, and would benefit only some households that fall below the income threshold. What is not captured in the simulations is the labor-market effect of the measures. It is quite likely that some (many?) GYED recipients will return to work—assuming that they have a job to return to, and someone to take care of their children. In this case, the poverty impact would be less—even positive. For those who do not (cannot) return to work, the situation could be quite bleak. A single female parent with one young child, for example, would receive around HUF 12,000 monthly (a minimum pension plus the family allowance for one child). This is not to argue against the reform measures, but merely to point out the inadequacy of the amount. Policymakers should consider increasing the amount, or alternatively, bringing these women under the umbrella of social assistance, as well as taking measure to improve child care provision for the needy, and to promote part-time employment for mothers with young children.

---

[7] "Technical Workshop on Policies for the Long-Term Unemployed in Hungary." Joint OECD/Hungarian Ministry of Labor, Budapest, January 1995.

## Reforming the Network of Social Assistance Programs

All told, almost 20 different cash programs constitute Hungary's social assistance system, although two-thirds of payments come from four programs—child rearing assistance (GYET), income support for the long-term unemployed, transitory assistance and regular social assistance. (In addition, there are more than a dozen in-kind social assistance programs.) With such a large number of programs that have evolved mostly unsystematically, coordination has become difficult, and the system is operationally inconsistent.

This study finds the various local-level social assistance programs the most progressive of Hungary's cash transfer programs, but they have proved to be the least effective at alleviating poverty. Social assistance programs have two major problems. First, they have serious benefit "leakages" and omissions. According to the 1993 Household Budget Survey, one-quarter of social assistance payments go to people whose incomes are above the subsistence minimum, including the socio- economic group that has the highest income of all—sole proprietors. (TARKI data corroborate this finding.) In part such leakage reflects the high income cut-off for certain social assistance programs (for example, GYET), but it also reflects the difficulties inherent in means testing, due to the close proximity of incomes, substantial grey and black-economy activities, and other devices to hide income. At the other extreme, 61 percent of households whose income/expenditure are less than the minimum pension do not receive any social assistance payment at all. In part this is likely a result of non-declaration. The other major problem is the low level of social assistance payments in general (an average of HUF 1,500 monthly per recipient household) and the large variation in payment levels both from one case to another, and from one local authority to another. In particular, the level of payments bear little relationship to need: in some cases, wealthier households receive payments that are larger than those going to poor households. The system needs to be completely overhauled. As elsewhere with the cash transfers system, too many people are currently receiving too little social assistance to ensure any meaningful poverty reduction. Moreover, with the dismantling of some of the other cash transfer programs (the family allowance, GYED, and GYES), social assistance must play a greater role as the last layer of the social safety net. If it misses people, they have nowhere else to turn (other than private or non-governmental charity).

Some of the shortcomings of the social assistance system are embedded in the design of the 1993 Social Service Welfare Administration and Social Services Act (the Social Act for short). Others arise from inadequate financial resources allocated to social assistance, the fragmented nature of programs, and poor administration. There are three basic problems with the 1993 Social Act:

- The income ceiling for some of the social assistance programs is too high. For example, the child-rearing benefit (GYET) has a ceiling of three times the minimum pension per capita. More than 70 percent of the population have an income level below this ceiling. Housing benefits, at twice the minimum pension, apply to around 30 percent of the population. Given the large number of people with a legitimate entitlement and with limited budgets, the level of support provided in many situations is too little or nonexistent.

- Standards that exist for assessing eligibility are based on an inappropriate per capita measure, which does not account for intra-household economies of scale; standards are potentially too generous for large households and discriminate against small households. Some form of equivalence scale should be used as a remedy.

- Many of the social assistance programs do not have a minimum level of support stipulated by law; rather, it is entirely at the discretion of the local governments. As such, payment levels differ throughout the country; for example, after income and household composition is controlled for, the inhabitants of Budapest's District 1 receive payments that are more than three times those for the residents of Tiszaujvaros (a small town in the east of Hungary) (CSO 1994). This reflects the differences in strategies adopted by the local authorities, as well as different administrative and financial capacities: one is meeting the broad needs of many families, and the other is meeting the more specific needs of fewer families. But in neither locality are the needs of the lowest income households being met.[8]

Local government financing attempts to adopt an equalizing dimension through the block grant system, which accounts for demographic and social characteristics. Within the block grant, the social subsidy norm is weighted to reflect the labor active/inactive status of the population, the unemployment rate, and the income-earning capacity of the area. It is not clear, however, whether this weighting is sufficient to meet the different social assistance needs. Local government officials claim that these weights do not generate sufficiently differentiated funding levels, and that many local authorities are having serious difficulties in delivering even the programs mandated by law for which part local funding is required (especially social assistance for the long-term unemployed and house maintenance assistance, particularly in urban areas.) Various strategies are being adopted to pass would-be claimants to other local authorities. (One such strategy is to raise the minimum residency requirement in a particular local authority to, say, three or four years.)

*A Workable Program Model.* As the 1993 Act was being prepared much discussion surrounded the pros and cons of nationally mandated social assistance programs, with prescribed eligibility criteria and benefit levels, including possibly a nationally prescribed minimum income for all. Although introducing entitlements for certain groups of the population, the 1993 Act stopped well short of providing a guaranteed minimum income for all due in large part to affordability. What exists, therefore, is a mixture of some modern, Western approaches to social assistance, overlaid on subjective, case-by-case eligibility criteria that are remnants of the previous system.

Further reform of social assistance programs should capitalize on the experience gained in recent years as well as on the indications on the features of poverty as discussed in this report. In this respect, the categories of citizens entitled to a nationally mandated social assistance program could be extended to include others with a high probability of belonging to poor segments of society. Benefits should then be set at levels ensuring that beneficiaries are lifted above the lower poverty line, but without creating undue disincentives to work. The system would have to be administratively simple so that benefit levels can be made more substantial and the potential target groups reached more effectively.

---

[8]     "No material correlation was found between the income position of and the (social assistance) subsidy amounts granted to families. Contrary to the preliminary assumption, however, it is not the lowest income families that receive the highest subsidy, but the families being in the most advantageous income position." (CSO 1994)

This advancement would require addressing several design issues:

- Which groups should be added -- the elderly without a pension entitlement could easily be added to the existing groups -- but who else?

- What is the minimum level to be set?

- Should the minimum be determined at the national level, local level, or a combination?

- How should the minimum be adjusted to account for household size—by per capita measures or equivalency?

- What should be the income ceiling governing eligibility -- less than at present for GYET, more than the minimum pension?

- Should eligibility be determined by local authorities, a national body, or a combination?

- How should eligibility be measured—mean tests of income,income/assets, or other characteristics (such as unemployment and/or housing status)?

- Who will bear the cost? - will it be shared between the local government and the central budget? Will more be funded centrally?

A less ambitious approach would be to promote the general concept of means-tested income minimums but allow individual local authorities to specify them according to their budgetary resources. This strategy would rest devolved administrative responsibility with local governments, making operations more consistent than under a more centralized approach. Yet it would leave scope for different standards—one of the major problems that already afflicts the social assistance system.

*Who should assume financing responsibility?* If responsibility for assessing assistance is to remain at the local level, some of the cost of financing the programs should remain there too. Otherwise, local authorities will have every incentive to accept all claims, since the cost will be entirely met by the center. Yet, giving local authorities too much financial responsibility would continue to prompt local authorities to do their best at minimizing expenditure on social assistance programs. A compromise position should be established, whereby local authorities have incentives to be efficient and effective with social assistance payments, but not frugal to the point of failing to address poverty alleviation. As is the practice in Hungary for support to the long-term unemployed, most countries adopt a cost-sharing arrangement between the local government and the central government. Differential cost-sharing arrangements could be envisaged for different categories of the population—for example, social assistance for the elderly could be reimbursed at a higher percentage than are pensions of working age people. But in any event, greater resources in the form of the block grant must be transferred to local governments to enable them to meet their additional funding obligations.

The size and administrative capacity of local governments vary tremendously. Some are quite capable of administering professional programs and effectively; others are not. Any policy reform that places more responsibility on the shoulders of local governments should also have measures to strengthen their capacity to administer. In some circumstances, it might make sense to stratify the capacity of local governments and to distribute functions to different levels of government. Personnel should also receive training in modern program operating techniques.

## Areas for Further Work

This report has shed light on several issues that fell outside its specific terms of reference. A more comprehensive understanding of the determinants of poverty in Hungary and more precise policy recommendations will require further work. Several areas of analysis are salient:

- The links between the labor market and poverty are critical, calling for a thorough analysis of the labor market—trends in employment, wages, unemployment, and withdrawal from the labor force—and feeding into labor market policy perspectives that address the alleviation of poverty.

- Education and training are emerging as major determinants of poverty particularly as they are requirements in the labor market. A study of access to and participation in education and training among both children and adults would probe both the static and dynamic (intergenerational) phenomena of poverty.

- Income from the black and grey economies has almost certainly cushioned the decline in formal market economy incomes and social transfers. Work to-date has indicated the magnitude of income from activities in the hidden economy, but little is known about the distribution of those incomes. From an anti-poverty policy stance, this knowledge would be very helpful.

- A related issue is the need to examine the distribution of unrecorded incomes in the 1993 HBS. The type of work that was done by Revesz on the 1989 and 1991 HBSs should be repeated.

- The situation of single mothers on extended childcare arrangements (GYED, GYES, and GYET) seems particularly precarious, and the March 1995 reform measures are potentially quite harmful to this group (who number around 260,000 mothers). A special study of this group, and an assessment of the impact of the reform measures on their situation, would be constructive.

- The TARKI panel, now four years old (1992-1995), is a rich data set that can tell a great deal about the dynamics of poverty and the movement of people in and out of poverty, around the poverty line, and into deeper poverty. This data set should be fully exploited as a panel to provide further insight into these questions.

# REFERENCES

Andorka, R., Z. Speder, and I. Toth. 1995. "Development in Poverty and Income Inequalities in Hungary, 1992-1994." Budapest: TARKI. (mimeo)

Arvay, J. and Vertes, A. 1993. "Size of the Hidden Economy". Preliminary Report. Budapest.

Central Statistical Office, 1993. "Some Characteristics of the Population Living Below the Subsistence Minimum". Budapest.

Central Statistical Office, 1994. "Social Welfare Services of the Local Government". Working document no.1. Budapest.

Deaton, A. and J. Muelbauer. 1980. *Economics and Consumer Behavior*. Cambridge: Cambridge University Press.

Fabian, Z. 1994. "Review of the Social Science Research into Poverty in Hungary". Budapest, TARKI. (mimeo)

Grootaert, C. 1995. "Poverty and Social Transfers in Poland." Policy Research Working Paper, No. 1440. Washington D.C.: The World Bank.

Grootaert, C., and R. Kanbur. 1990. "Policy-oriented Analysis of Poverty and the Social Dimensions of Structural Adjustment - A Methodology and Proposed Application to Cote d'Ivoire, 1985-88." Social Dimensions of Adjustment Working Paper No. 1. Washington, D.C.: The World Bank.

Jarvis, S. and Micklewright, J. 1992. "The Targeting of Family Allowance in Hungary". Paper prepared for World Bank Conference on Public Expenditure and the Poor: Incidence and Targeting. Washington D.C.

Kanbur, R. 1987. "Measurement and Alleviation of Poverty." *IMF Staff Papers*, Vol. 34, No. 1.

Kertesi, G. et.al. 1994. "The Education and Employment Situation in the Gypsy Community: Report of the 1993/94 National Sample Survey". ILO/Japan Project on Employment Policies for Transition in Hungary, Working paper No. 17, Budapest.

Milanovic, B. 1992. "Poverty in Eastern Europe in the Years of Crisis, 1978 to 1987: Poland, Hungary, and Yugoslavia". *World Bank Economic Review*, Vol. 5 (2).

Milanovic, B. 1995. "Poverty, Inequality and Social Policy in Transition Economies". World Bank Research Paper Series Paper No. 9. Washington D.C.

Ministry of Finance. 1993. "New Regulations on Social Insurance and Other Social Benefits." *Public Finance in Hungary*, No. 120. Budapest.

OECD. 1994. "The Jobs Study".

Revesz, T. 1994. "An Analysis of the Representativity of the Hungarian Household Budget Survey Samples". Department of Applied Economies, University of Cambridge. (mimeo)

Szivos, P. 1994. "Evolution of Poverty in Hungary, 1987-1992". Budapest: Central Statistical Office. (mimeo)

Szivos, P. 1995. "Profile of Poverty in Hungary, 1993". Budapest: Central Statistical Office. (mimeo)

TARKI, 1995. "Social Changes, Poverty and the Distribution of Social Incomes among Strata of Society". Budapest. (mimeo)

Toth, I., R. Andorka, M. Forster, and Z. Speder. 1994. "Poverty, Inequalities and the Incidence of Social Transfers in Hungary, 1992-1993". Budapest: TARKI. (mimeo)

Van De Walle, D., M. Ravallion, and M. Gautam. 1994. "How Well Does the Social Safety Net Work? The Incidence of Cash Benefits in Hungary, 1987-1989". Living Standards Measurement Study Working Paper, No. 102. Washington, D.C.: The World Bank.

World Bank. 1995. "Hungary - Structural Reforms for Sustainable Growth". World Bank, Washington, D.C.

World Bank. 1992. "Hungary - Reform of Social Policy and Expenditure." A World Bank Country Study. Washington, D.C.

World Bank. 1995. "Poverty and Vulnerability in Angyalfold, Hungary". Urban Development Division, Washington D.C.

## Annex 1: Poverty Before the Transition

In Hungary, as throughout much of Central and Eastern Europe, the study of poverty and social inequality was prohibited for decades on ideological grounds. Yet work was carried out -- often behind closed doors -- and in recent years findings have been made available.[1] In the late 1960s, around 1 million Hungarians -- 10 percent of the population -- were found to be in poverty (below the minimum subsistence level), and another 1.5 million close to poverty (below the somewhat higher socially acceptable minimum). In addition to old age persons who were known to be poorly off (especially those living in remote locations), research of the late 1960s found a new poverty phenomenon -- workers and their families, not only those engaged in agriculture and having irregular employment, but also those with regular jobs. This phenomenon challenged one of the basic principles of socialism. Another dimension of poverty that emerged during this period was the vulnerability of an important ethnic minority group -- the gypsies, who through the combination of low education, low skill, marginal labor market status and large number of children were found to be substantially over-represented in the lowest income groups. Moreover, low school attainment of gypsy children -- and indeed children of other unskilled workers[2] -- was considered to be a key determinant of inter-generational poverty.

After a decade of repression, research on poverty emerged again in the 1980s. Observers of poverty in the early 1980s (e.g. Ferge) noted the absence of "traditional poverty", citing hunger, mass squalor, precarious living conditions and general scarcity as features of the past. Instead, notions of relative poverty and relative deprivation became more the order of the day. Broadly three strata of society were identified: the privileged, the middle stratum and the deprived. A key factor affecting the relative income position of households was the extent to which they participated in the second (private) economy. Around 1.5 million people were recorded as "deprived" in the early 1980s, and their characteristics differed little from the 1960s: the elderly, inactive dependents, the poorly educated and unskilled who held low paying and/or irregular jobs, and those living in remote parts of the country. By the end of the 1980s, however, those in poverty were somewhat different in characteristic. Of significance was the shift in poverty from rural locations to urban dwellers, and from pensioners and the inactive to young working families.

---

[1]     For a good synopsis of past research on poverty see: Fabian, Zoltan. " Review of the Social Science Research into Poverty in Hungary". Background paper commissioned by the World Bank, Budapest, November 1994.

[2]     Around 20 percent of children in families where the household head was an unskilled worker failed to complete primary school at this time.

## Table A1.1: Ratio of those living below the subsistence minima, 1977-87

| | all households | Households with active earners | Households without active earners |
|---|---|---|---|
| **a. From Income Surveys** | | | |
| 1977(a) | 11.7 | 10.7 | 18.0 |
| 1982 | 10.3 | 10.0 | 11.9 |
| 1987 | 12.7 | 13.5 | 8.5 |
| **b. From Household Budget Surveys** | | | |
| 1978(a) | 15.4 | 14.4 | 21.1 |
| 1980(a) | 13.8 | 13.2 | 17.2 |
| 1982 | 14.8 | 15.0 | 13.3 |
| 1983 | 16.7 | 16.5 | 18.0 |
| 1985 | 15.7 | 16.0 | 14.2 |
| 1987 | 13.8 | 14.5 | 10.5 |

*Source*: CSO Statistical Yearbooks; "Some Characteristics of the Population Living Below the Subsistence Minimum", special publication of the CSO, Budapest, July 1993.

*Note*: (a) Subsistence minima calculated retrospectively by CSO back to 1982. Values for 1977, 1978 and 1980 are estimates based on the assumption that the ratio of the national subsistence minima to the average monthly per capita income was the same for those years as for 1982.

## Annex 2: Data and Methodological Considerations

This study utilizes two data sources: the 1993 Household Budget Survey (HBS) and the 1992-93-94 Household Panel Survey (HPS).[1] The 1993 HBS, which is the main data source, is part of a tradition of budget surveys undertaken by the Central Statistical Office (CSO) since the early 1950s. The surveys are conducted every two years, and 1993 is the first HBS which fully incorporates western economic concepts. The 1993 sample is about 9000 households, selected in a two-stage stratified design, and covering the whole non-institutional population in Hungary.

The HPS is a panel survey conducted by TARKI (Social Research Informatics Center), aimed at following changes in the social and economic conditions of Hungarian households. The HPS's main advantage is that it follows the same households over time and thus permits to study the dynamics of poverty. It is this feature of the data which is utilized in this report. The drawback is that the sample size is only 2000 households, so that the amount of disaggregation in the analysis is limited.

The most important methodological point to be addressed is whether household income or expenditure should be used as the basis for the analysis. Most previous work on poverty and social transfers in Hungary has relied on income (for example, see Szivos, 1994, Toth et al., 1994, Milanovic, 1991). The main reason for this was the high quality of income data in past Hungarian household surveys, stemming in part from the fact that wages in the state sector and public transfers used to be the main sources of income and these could easily be cross-checked at the firm or state level. With the transition away from a command economy and central planning this has changed, and private sector incomes have grown in importance. It is well known that there is a large "black" or "grey" economy operating in Hungary, which largely escapes taxation and recording in official statistics. Even fully legal and known own account activities are often missed in household income surveys. In a detailed comparison of survey income figures with macro-economic aggregates, Revesz (1994) found that wage earnings were fairly well reported in the 1989 and 1991 HBS (91 percent and 86 percent of the macro-total, respectively), but self-employment income was under-reported by as much as 80 percent.

A similar analysis is underway for the 1993 HBS, and preliminary results suggest that the problem of under-reported income from own account activities has remained. In addition, under-reporting of *private sector* wages and salaries has become an additional problem. (Wages and salaries in the HBS account for 70 percent of the macro figures.) According to Table A2.1, average reported household income and expenditure (adjusted for the size and composition of households - see below) in the 1993 HBS are identical. This is the case in Budapest as well as in the rest of the country. There are however some differences according to socio-economic category. For groups where wages and pensions are the main sources of income, the difference between average income and expenditure is small. For the self-employed and sole proprietors, expenditure exceeds income by almost 30 percent, most likely as a result of under-reported income. For poorer groups, such as households headed by an unemployed person or those relying on child care benefits as main source of income, expenditure exceeds income probably as a direct result of the low level of income, necessitating borrowing or dis-saving.

This equality between average household income and expenditure in the HBS results raises questions because it does not correspond to the economic reality as captured in the national accounts. According to these, total household consumption was roughly 1900 billion HUF and total household

---

[1]    A fourth wave is now available, but is not reflected in this report.

income was 2200 billion HUF, implying an aggregate saving rate of about 14 percent (see Szivos, 1995).

There is a further disturbing result in the 1993 HBS data. The results suggest that the distribution of household expenditure per equivalent adult is more unequal than the distribution of household income per equivalent adult. Annex Table 3.1 (upper part) shows this. Figure 1.2 plots the distribution. (Annex Table 3.1 also shows that when individuals are ranked by income rather than expenditure, significant rank reversals occur.)

**Table A2.1: Average Household Expenditure and Disposable Income per equivalent adult (HUF per year), 1993**

|  | Household expenditure per equivalent adult | Household income per equivalent adult | Expenditure as percentage of income |
|---|---|---|---|
| Budapest | 200,598 | 201,690 | 99.5% |
| Towns | 183,801 | 182,944 | 100.5% |
| Villages | 171,284 | 171,263 | 100.0% |
| Permanent employee | 200,996 | 204,861 | 98.1% |
| Temporary employee | 133,401 | 133,130 | 100.2% |
| Self-employed | 227,440 | 179,542 | 126.7% |
| Sole proprietor | 267,701 | 207,277 | 129.2% |
| Unemployed | 136,548 | 120,267 | 113.5% |
| Pensioner | 155,807 | 158,844 | 98.1% |
| Child care receiver | 170,008 | 139,388 | 122.0% |
| Other | 165,618 | 155,434 | 106.6% |
| Country | 182,771 | 182,643 | 100.1% |

Observations from almost all countries - developed and developing - suggest that the distribution of expenditure is more equal than that of income because typically the rich save and the poor (and often the middle classes) dis-save. If the HBS results correspond to economic reality, the reverse would be true in Hungary. Since income is disposable income, it would mean that the income tax system is very progressive in Hungary to the point of pulling the highest incomes below expenditure, while at the same time the social transfer system is so generous that it pushes the income of the poor above their expenditure level. Alternatively, the HBS results could reflect reporting errors, in particular under-reporting of income by the rich and under-reporting of expenditure by the poor. The former is very likely, and consistent with the numbers in Table A2.1. Evidence in Hungary as well as in other transition economies suggests that private sector incomes have the most unequal distribution, and these are the incomes which the rich are likely to hide. Under-reporting of expenditures by the poor is less self-evident, but it is possible, to the extent that people with low education, the elderly, and others who may have difficulty reporting expenditures accurately are concentrated among the poor. Such difficulties could arise in filling out the HBS diary forms or simply in recalling expenditures.

The selection of income or expenditure as measure of household living standard will thus have an impact on calculated poverty statistics as well as on indicators of the targeting of social transfers. The difference could be significant. Figure 1.2 shows that up to a benchmark of approximately 200,000 HUF/year, the selection of expenditure as the criterion will lead to higher poverty estimates than if income is selected. Moreover, households are ranked differently by the two distributions: the Pearson correlation coefficient between household income and expenditure is 0.71.[2] This means that the pattern of poverty will not be the same with the two criteria. In order to assess the extent of this the poverty profile tables were recalculated using net household income as the criterion. When using a relative poverty line (2/3 of mean household income per equivalent adult) the differences with the expenditure based poverty profile were minimal -- very few rank reversals occurred among the categories of households. In the case of the minimum pension poverty line, rank reversals were, however, more frequent. In particular, people living in towns, single female adults, households were the head had less than primary education, child care receivers, and the aged had lower poverty incidence with income than with expenditure criterion. It is normal that sensitivity to the criterion is higher for lower poverty lines, especially a line such as the minimum pension which, in the case of income, only cuts off 2.5 percent of the population.

All this shows that there are some problems with the HBS data, although it does not take away from the fact that it is the best data source available in Hungary to study poverty and social transfers. It should also be emphasized that such problems are by no means unique to the Hungarian HBS. In fact, they are typical of almost all household surveys which collect both household income and expenditure, although of course the extent of divergence between the two measures differs. Practically, the existence of these data imperfections does not absolve one from deciding whether to use income or expenditure as the basis of the analysis. The choice has been to use expenditure for two reasons:

- There are strong and well-known theoretical advantages to using household expenditure for poverty analysis, because it is deemed to reflect better permanent income (for example, see Deaton and Muellbauer, 1980);

- The weight of evidence, from the 1993 HBS as well as from earlier HBS, suggests that the reporting problems are more severe with income. This pertains especially to private sector income. (However, it is clear that further research into this question is needed).

The use of household expenditure as the basis to measure the well-being of households requires that two factors be taken into account: household size and composition, and differences in prices faced by different households. The former has been done by expressing expenditure on a per equivalent adult basis. The OECD-scale has been used (first adult =1; other adults =0.7; children less than 14 years = 0.5). This scale corresponds closely to the one implicit in the calculation of subsistence minima by the CSO for different types of households. The question of regional price variation in different parts of Hungary has also been addressed. While no official statistics are available to that effect, the answer appears to be negative, which is plausible given that Hungary is a small country with good means of

---

[2]    This is actually a fairly high correlation as far as household survey data are concerned. In comparable data sets in other Central and East European and FSU Countries, correlations as low as 0.2 have been observed.

transportation.[3] Hence this study is based on nominal expenditure as collected in the survey. This is consistent with use of HBS data in Hungary (for example, see Szivos, 1995).

---

[3] A study for Poland found that regional price variation does not exceed 2% for the average consumption bundle as a whole (Grootaert, 1995).

# ANNEX 3: TABLES

## Table A3.1: Distribution of Disposable Household Income and Household Expenditure per Equivalent Adult (HUF/year)

### A) Expenditure Deciles
### (10% of persons)

| Decile | Household Expenditure per Equivalent Adult | Disposable Household Income per Equivalent Adult |
|:---:|:---:|:---:|
| 1 | 76,208 | 112,022 |
| 2 | 103,141 | 135,629 |
| 3 | 121,259 | 149,553 |
| 4 | 137,161 | 157,202 |
| 5 | 152,364 | 168,525 |
| 6 | 169,722 | 182,482 |
| 7 | 188,836 | 190,672 |
| 8 | 214,274 | 209,695 |
| 9 | 255,971 | 232,518 |
| 10 | 405,577 | 289,038 |
| Average | 182,317 | 182,679 |

### B) Income Deciles
### (10% of persons)

| Deciles | Disposable Household Income per Equivalent Adult | Household Expenditures per Equivalent Adult |
|:---:|:---:|:---:|
| 1 | 86,019 | 112,013 |
| 2 | 118,129 | 130,230 |
| 3 | 134,201 | 135,738 |
| 4 | 148,013 | 151,341 |
| 5 | 161,285 | 173,036 |
| 6 | 174,821 | 173,857 |
| 7 | 191,439 | 186,539 |
| 8 | 214,198 | 204,148 |
| 9 | 247,474 | 238,632 |
| 10 | 351,371 | 317,764 |
| Average | 182,679 | 182,317 |

**Table A3.2: The Composition of Household Income (percentage)**

| | Wage income | Self-employment income | Property income | Social transfers | Private transfers | Other income | Total | Mean gross income (HUF/year) | Taxes and contributions | Transfers | Disposable income as a percentage of gross income |
|---|---|---|---|---|---|---|---|---|---|---|---|
| Budapest | 61.8 | 6.4 | 0.3 | 28.0 | 2.4 | 1.2 | 100.0 | 520,620 | 21.5 | 1.6 | 76.9 |
| Towns | 56.4 | 9.9 | 0.3 | 29.3 | 3.0 | 1.2 | 100.0 | 490,739 | 17.8 | 1.7 | 80.5 |
| Villages | 46.2 | 15.0 | 0.5 | 34.5 | 2.3 | 1.5 | 100.0 | 445,633 | 13.3 | 1.7 | 85.0 |
| 1 Male adult | 45.6 | 14.0 | 0.5 | 37.0 | 1.2 | 1.6 | 100.0 | 235,404 | 16.5 | 4.9 | 78.6 |
| 1 Female adult | 23.3 | 6.6 | 0.8 | 64.3 | 3.4 | 1.6 | 100.0 | 178,059 | 8.0 | 3.1 | 88.9 |
| 1 Adult with children | 53.2 | 5.1 | 0.1 | 29.2 | 11.3 | 1.1 | 100.0 | 350,888 | 15.0 | 1.4 | 83.7 |
| 2+ Adults | 51.8 | 10.5 | 0.4 | 34.4 | 1.7 | 1.2 | 100.0 | 495,094 | 16.5 | 1.9 | 81.6 |
| 2 Adults with 1-2 children | 64.1 | 11.3 | 0.2 | 19.0 | 4.1 | 1.3 | 100.0 | 592,069 | 19.9 | 1.4 | 78.7 |
| 2 Adults with 3 children | 53.5 | 9.6 | 0.3 | 32.5 | 2.7 | 1.4 | 100.0 | 643,664 | 16.5 | 0.8 | 82.6 |
| 2 Adults with 4+ children | 36.7 | 8.0 | 0.0 | 53.2 | 1.0 | 1.1 | 100.0 | 541,688 | 9.4 | 0.4 | 90.2 |
| 3+ Adults with 1-2 children | 58.6 | 13.7 | 0.3 | 24.4 | 1.8 | 1.2 | 100.0 | 710,811 | 18.6 | 0.9 | 80.5 |
| 3+ Adults with 3+ children | 33.2 | 5.7 | 0.0 | 54.8 | 3.3 | 3.0 | 100.0 | 609,271 | 8.1 | 0.6 | 91.4 |
| Below min. pension | 29.1 | 6.6 | 0.2 | 61.3 | 1.5 | 1.3 | 100.0 | 253,602 | 6.2 | 1.1 | 92.7 |
| Btwn min. pension and 2/3 mean exp. | 38.5 | 8.6 | 0.2 | 49.9 | 1.7 | 1.1 | 100.0 | 319,448 | 9.6 | 1.7 | 88.6 |
| Between 2/3 mean exp. and subsistence min. | 49.5 | 10.0 | 0.2 | 37.2 | 2.1 | 1.0 | 100.0 | 418,523 | 14.1 | 1.7 | 84.2 |
| Above subsistence min. | 61.6 | 12.0 | 0.5 | 21.3 | 3.2 | 1.5 | 100.0 | 634,653 | 21.0 | 1.7 | 77.3 |

**Table A3.2: The Composition of Household Income (percentage) (continued)**

| | Wage income | Self-employment income | Property income | Social transfers | Private transfers | Other income | Total | Mean gross income (HUF/year) | Taxes and contributions | Transfers | Disposable income as a percentage of gross income |
|---|---|---|---|---|---|---|---|---|---|---|---|
| Permanent employee | 70.7 | 8.2 | 0.3 | 17.1 | 2.6 | 1.2 | 100.0 | 640,724 | 21.7 | 1.4 | 76.9 |
| Temporary employee | 44.6 | 6.9 | 0.4 | 35.5 | 11.7 | 0.9 | 100.0 | 314,576 | 3.8 | 1.1 | 95.1 |
| Self employed | 24.2 | 51.3 | 1.3 | 19.1 | 2.2 | 2.0 | 100.0 | 544,471 | 16.5 | 1.6 | 81.9 |
| Sole proprietor | 24.6 | 60.2 | 0.8 | 12.4 | 1.6 | 0.3 | 100.0 | 758,746 | 24.7 | 1.1 | 74.2 |
| Unemployed | 15.5 | 11.9 | 0.2 | 65.9 | 4.1 | 2.4 | 100.0 | 298,214 | 4.6 | 1.4 | 94.0 |
| Pensioner | 4.3 | 9.0 | 0.6 | 83.0 | 1.9 | 1.4 | 100.0 | 251,258 | 1.4 | 2.9 | 95.6 |
| Child care receiver | 19.2 | 8.7 | 0.3 | 57.4 | 13.3 | 1.1 | 100.0 | 344,534 | 2.4 | 1.5 | 96.0 |
| Other | 45.3 | 9.7 | 0.6 | 35.3 | 5.4 | 3.6 | 100.0 | 366,944 | 10.9 | 1.4 | 87.6 |
| Less than primary | 12.1 | 10.8 | 0.2 | 73.8 | 1.8 | 1.3 | 100.0 | 230,359 | 2.9 | 2.7 | 94.3 |
| Primary | 42.6 | 10.8 | 0.7 | 43.0 | 1.6 | 1.4 | 100.0 | 377,833 | 11.2 | 1.8 | 86.9 |
| Secondary vocational | 59.1 | 13.1 | 0.3 | 22.6 | 4.0 | 0.9 | 100.0 | 552,667 | 17.4 | 1.5 | 81.1 |
| Special post primary | 58.7 | 7.6 | 0.2 | 30.2 | 1.9 | 1.4 | 100.0 | 432,899 | 15.2 | 1.7 | 83.1 |
| Secondary grammar | 56.6 | 10.1 | 0.4 | 28.5 | 2.8 | 1.6 | 100.0 | 518,733 | 18.0 | 1.6 | 80.4 |
| Other secondary | 62.3 | 10.7 | 0.3 | 23.2 | 2.3 | 1.2 | 100.0 | 596,892 | 20.9 | 1.5 | 77.6 |
| College | 69.2 | 7.8 | 0.2 | 19.2 | 2.3 | 1.2 | 100.0 | 705,002 | 24.4 | 1.7 | 73.9 |
| University | 68.4 | 8.4 | 0.3 | 18.5 | 2.4 | 1.9 | 100.0 | 815,036 | 26.6 | 1.7 | 71.8 |
| All | 54.1 | 10.8 | 0.4 | 30.8 | 2.6 | 1.3 | 100.0 | 480,431 | 17.1 | 1.7 | 81.2 |

Table A3.3: The Composition of Social Transfers (percentage)

| | Pension | Unemployment benefit | Family allowance | Child care allowance | Social assistance | Child care fee | All social transfers |
|---|---|---|---|---|---|---|---|
| Budapest | 71.0 | 5.6 | 16.2 | 1.7 | 2.9 | 2.6 | 100.0 |
| Towns | 62.0 | 8.4 | 22.1 | 1.9 | 3.0 | 2.7 | 100.0 |
| Villages | 61.2 | 10.9 | 20.1 | 2.4 | 2.7 | 2.7 | 100.0 |
| 1 Male adult | 89.5 | 8.6 | - | - | 1.7 | - | 100.0 |
| 1 Female adult | 97.5 | 1.0 | - | - | 1.5 | - | 100.0 |
| 1 Adult with children | 12.6 | 7.9 | 62.6 | 4.6 | 10.3 | 2.0 | 100.0 |
| 2+ Adults | 84.8 | 7.4 | 5.4 | 0.0 | 1.8 | 0.6 | 100.0 |
| 2 Adults with 1-2 children | 9.7 | 16.8 | 51.8 | 8.0 | 3.6 | 10.2 | 100.0 |
| 2 Adults with 3 children | 3.8 | 7.1 | 63.8 | 8.5 | 6.2 | 10.6 | 100.0 |
| 2 Adults with 4+ children | 1.3 | 6.6 | 69.0 | 7.5 | 10.4 | 5.1 | 100.0 |
| 3+ Adults with 1-2 children | 33.9 | 11.8 | 43.7 | 2.9 | 4.5 | 3.0 | 100.0 |
| 3+ Adults with 3+ children | 22.4 | 9.8 | 46.6 | 3.9 | 13.3 | 3.9 | 100.0 |
| Below min. pension | 52.3 | 14.3 | 21.2 | 3.4 | 6.6 | 2.1 | 100.0 |
| Btwn min. pension and 2/3 mean exp. | 65.6 | 10.5 | 17.0 | 2.0 | 3.4 | 1.5 | 100.0 |
| Btwn 2/3 mean exp. and subsistence min. | 65.9 | 8.3 | 18.8 | 2.0 | 2.7 | 2.3 | 100.0 |
| Above subsistence min. | 61.5 | 7.5 | 22.9 | 92.0 | 2.3 | 3.9 | 100.0 |
| Permanent employee | 37.8 | 11.2 | 38.5 | 3.8 | 3.6 | 5.2 | 100.0 |
| Temporary employee | 34.8 | 12.1 | 35.9 | 0.9 | 13.7 | 2.7 | 100.0 |
| Self employed | 34.1 | 9.8 | 43.7 | 4.0 | 2.9 | 5.4 | 100.0 |
| Sole proprietor | 21.2 | 5.4 | 54.3 | 5.8 | 10.1 | 3.2 | 100.0 |
| Unemployed | 15.4 | 43.9 | 25.9 | 4.0 | 6.0 | 4.7 | 100.0 |
| Pensioner | 94.6 | 1.9 | 1.9 | 0.1 | 1.4 | 0.1 | 100.0 |
| Child care receiver | 14.8 | 14.1 | 42.7 | 12.3 | 3.9 | 12.1 | 100.0 |
| Other | 39.1 | 23.6 | 20.9 | 3.2 | 10.1 | 3.1 | 100.0 |
| Less than primary | 88.9 | 3.7 | 4.3 | 0.3 | 2.4 | 0.4 | 100.0 |
| Primary | 70.8 | 9.0 | 14.8 | 1.5 | 2.9 | 1.1 | 100.0 |
| Secondary vocational | 34.3 | 14.4 | 37.2 | 4.9 | 4.1 | 5.0 | 100.0 |
| Special post primary | 58.9 | 13.7 | 18.9 | 3.4 | 1.2 | 3.9 | 100.0 |
| Secondary grammar | 65.7 | 7.2 | 21.1 | 1.1 | 3.4 | 1.5 | 100.0 |
| Other secondary | 57.2 | 9.6 | 24.4 | 2.4 | 2.1 | 4.3 | 100.0 |
| College | 60.4 | 5.7 | 26.8 | 1.3 | 2.4 | 3.4 | 100.0 |
| University | 62.8 | 5.8 | 19.8 | 2.1 | 1.5 | 8.1 | 100.0 |
| All | 63.6 | 8.7 | 20.1 | 2.1 | 2.8 | 2.7 | 100.0 |

Table A3.4: The Composition of Household Expenditure (percentage)

| | Food | Beverages and tobacco | Clothing and footwear | Housing | Housing maintenance | Medical and health expenses | Transportation and communication | Education, recreation | Construction, purchase of dwellings | Other expenses | Total expenses | Total exp. (HUF/year) |
|---|---|---|---|---|---|---|---|---|---|---|---|---|
| Budapest | 31.2 | 6.0 | 7.1 | 13.5 | 5.3 | 5.0 | 14.1 | 7.5 | 7.1 | 3.2 | 100.0 | 399,104 |
| Towns | 32.8 | 5.6 | 8.1 | 15.0 | 5.7 | 4.0 | 12.8 | 6.4 | 6.4 | 3.2 | 100.0 | 394,110 |
| Villages | 36.3 | 6.3 | 7.1 | 13.6 | 5.7 | 3.0 | 12.8 | 4.7 | 7.7 | 2.7 | 100.0 | 377,344 |
| 1 Male adult | 34.8 | 10.4 | 5.0 | 17.1 | 4.6 | 3.6 | 12.0 | 6.2 | 3.0 | 3.5 | 100.0 | 199,575 |
| 1 Female adult | 37.2 | 3.7 | 4.8 | 23.6 | 6.1 | 5.5 | 5.9 | 5.1 | 4.8 | 3.3 | 100.0 | 162,784 |
| 1 Adult with children | 32.4 | 3.9 | 9.5 | 16.7 | 5.2 | 3.2 | 9.0 | 7.6 | 10.1 | 2.3 | 100.0 | 322,701 |
| 2+ Adults | 34.9 | 6.5 | 6.7 | 14.4 | 5.7 | 4.2 | 12.7 | 5.7 | 6.0 | 3.2 | 100.0 | 388,573 |
| 2 Adults with 1-2 children | 30.5 | 5.4 | 8.8 | 12.5 | 5.7 | 3.4 | 15.4 | 6.7 | 8.7 | 2.8 | 100.0 | 488,743 |
| 2 Adults with 3 children | 33.2 | 5.7 | 7.7 | 12.2 | 5.2 | 3.1 | 12.2 | 6.2 | 12.3 | 2.2 | 100.0 | 553,108 |
| 2 Adults with 4 + children | 41.5 | 5.5 | 9.5 | 12.4 | 6.4 | 3.9 | 4.5 | 5.2 | 8.2 | 2.9 | 100.0 | 442,495 |
| 3 + Adults with 1-2 children | 33.9 | 5.7 | 8.9 | 12.1 | 5.2 | 3.1 | 14.5 | 6.3 | 7.2 | 3.2 | 100.0 | 566,333 |
| 3 + Adults with 3 + children | 43.7 | 9.0 | 7.4 | 11.5 | 6.1 | 3.1 | 7.0 | 4.2 | 5.3 | 2.8 | 100.0 | 482,599 |
| Below min. pension | 49.8 | 8.1 | 5.5 | 18.7 | 3.9 | 3.9 | 2.7 | 3.6 | 2.3 | 1.4 | 100.0 | 149,203 |
| Btwn min. pension and 2/3 mean exp. | 44.9 | 7.6 | 6.0 | 18.5 | 4.4 | 4.0 | 5.1 | 4.2 | 3.1 | 2.3 | 100.0 | 214,261 |
| Btwn 2/3 mean exp. and subsistence min. | 39.5 | 6.8 | 7.1 | 16.9 | 5.0 | 3.9 | 8.8 | 5.3 | 4.0 | 2.7 | 100.0 | 313,302 |
| Above subsistence min. | 28.6 | 5.2 | 8.0 | 11.9 | 6.2 | 3.8 | 16.8 | 6.8 | 9.3 | 3.4 | 100.0 | 562,545 |

# Table A3.4: The Composition of Household Expenditure (percentage) (continued)

| | Food | Beverages and tobacco | Clothing and footwear | Housing | Housing maintenance | Medical and health expenses | Transportation and communication | Education, recreation | Construction, purchase of dwellings | Other expenses | Total expenses | Total exp. (HUF/year) |
|---|---|---|---|---|---|---|---|---|---|---|---|---|
| Permanent employee | 31.8 | 6.0 | 8.4 | 12.9 | 5.6 | 3.6 | 14.9 | 6.7 | 6.9 | 3.2 | 100.0 | 481,424 |
| Temporary employee | 41.2 | 11.0 | 7.3 | 12.1 | 3.3 | 4.1 | 11.1 | 3.3 | 5.1 | 1.4 | 100.0 | 295,082 |
| Self employed | 28.3 | 4.8 | 7.9 | 11.3 | 6.0 | 3.3 | 17.6 | 6.3 | 11.3 | 3.3 | 100.0 | 570,866 |
| Sole proprietor | 26.7 | 5.9 | 7.1 | 11.4 | 6.0 | 4.1 | 25.3 | 5.8 | 2.7 | 5.0 | 100.0 | 699,835 |
| Unemployed | 39.2 | 7.8 | 6.6 | 15.0 | 5.2 | 3.6 | 7.0 | 4.3 | 9.3 | 1.7 | 100.0 | 309,657 |
| Pensioner | 40.6 | 5.9 | 4.7 | 18.8 | 5.9 | 4.9 | 6.6 | 4.5 | 5.5 | 2.7 | 100.0 | 232,912 |
| Child care receiver | 31.8 | 4.4 | 5.8 | 13.9 | 5.1 | 3.4 | 6.6 | 2.8 | 24.4 | 1.9 | 100.0 | 386,455 |
| Other | 34.0 | 6.0 | 7.8 | 17.2 | 4.9 | 5.0 | 9.6 | 5.2 | 7.9 | 2.5 | 100.0 | 331,689 |
| Less than primary | 44.6 | 6.6 | 4.9 | 18.3 | 5.9 | 4.5 | 4.1 | 3.2 | 5.5 | 2.5 | 100.0 | 203,048 |
| Primary | 39.4 | 7.1 | 6.6 | 15.9 | 5.4 | 3.6 | 8.6 | 5.1 | 5.4 | 3.0 | 100.0 | 313,339 |
| Secondary vocational | 33.8 | 6.5 | 8.1 | 13.5 | 5.6 | 3.4 | 13.3 | 5.7 | 7.0 | 3.1 | 100.0 | 448,921 |
| Special post primary | 33.0 | 7.2 | 7.8 | 14.6 | 4.4 | 5.1 | 9.2 | 6.0 | 9.8 | 3.1 | 100.0 | 344,284 |
| Secondary grammar | 30.7 | 5.2 | 7.6 | 13.9 | 5.5 | 4.0 | 12.5 | 6.9 | 10.9 | 2.8 | 100.0 | 434,207 |
| Other secondary | 30.0 | 5.2 | 7.8 | 13.0 | 5.9 | 3.8 | 17.0 | 6.9 | 7.4 | 2.9 | 100.0 | 480,887 |
| College | 26.5 | 4.7 | 8.7 | 12.4 | 6.0 | 4.6 | 19.1 | 8.5 | 5.6 | 4.0 | 100.0 | 539,640 |
| University | 25.8 | 4.2 | 8.3 | 11.4 | 5.4 | 4.2 | 19.6 | 7.7 | 9.9 | 3.4 | 100.0 | 587,840 |
| All | 33.7 | 6.0 | 7.5 | 14.1 | 5.6 | 3.8 | 13.1 | 6.1 | 7.0 | 3.1 | 100.0 | 388,963 |

### Table A3.5: Incidence of Poverty among Children

| | Below minimum pension (6,400 HUF/mo) | Below 2/3 of mean expenditure (10,129 HUF/mo) |
|---|---|---|
| Budapest | 3.8% | 26.5% |
| Towns | 4.7% | 24.5% |
| Villages | 6.9% | 30.9% |
| Permanent employee | 2.9% | 21.6% |
| Temporary employee | 18.6% | 53.8% |
| Self employed | 2.3% | 22.8% |
| Sole proprietor | 0.0% | 6.0% |
| Unemployed | 19.6% | 63.7% |
| Pensioner | 12.6% | 51.8% |
| Child care receiver | 26.6% | 56.2% |
| Other | 9.4% | 31.7% |
| Male headed households | 4.5% | 26.0% |
| Female headed households | 9.8% | 33.6% |
| Education of head | | |
| Less than primary | 29.6% | 68.4% |
| Primary | 11.7% | 51.5% |
| Secondary vocational | 4.1% | 25.1% |
| Special post-primary | 7.1% | 31.8% |
| Secondary grammar | 0.7% | 18.3% |
| Other secondary | 1.0% | 14.3% |
| College | 0.9% | 4.9% |
| University | 0.0% | 2.1% |
| All | 5.4% | **27.4%** |

Table A3.6: Average Amount of Social Transfers (HUF/year) Received by Recipient Households

| | Pension | Unemployment benefit | Family allowance | Child care allowance | Social assistance | Child care fee | All social transfers |
|---|---|---|---|---|---|---|---|
| Below min. pension | 135,857 | 82,483 | 68,014 | 48,844 | 26,539 | 81,772 | 160,551 |
| Btwn min. pension and 2/3 of mean hhold exp. | 162,054 | 78,504 | 68,454 | 42,647 | 19,572 | 62,013 | 165,779 |
| Btwn 2/3 of mean hhold exp. and subsistence min. | 179,959 | 80,638 | 68,129 | 40,890 | 17,377 | 74,614 | 164,504 |
| Above subsistence min. | 200,310 | 79,427 | 65,361 | 42,347 | 16,343 | 105,151 | 158,353 |
| Budapest | 201,857 | 100,743 | 61,961 | 38,162 | 26,663 | 199,678 | 167,932 |
| Towns | 183,024 | 76,346 | 66,791 | 41,616 | 18,983 | 73,128 | 158,311 |
| Villages | 165,529 | 77,977 | 69,644 | 44,746 | 14,695 | 77,417 | 163,420 |
| 1 Male adult | 146,802 | 7,472 | - | - | 13,215 | - | 132,444 |
| 1 Female adult | 126,620 | 88,884 | - | - | 8,511 | - | 126,672 |
| 1 Adult with children | 95,477 | 68,193 | 66,515 | 40,415 | 23,587 | 59,954 | 104,093 |
| 2+ Adults | 212,589 | 79,557 | 47,181 | 39,468 | 17,658 | 252,459 | 195,428 |
| 2 Adults with 1-2 children | 123,884 | 83,546 | 59,052 | 40,974 | 14,646 | 79,552 | 113,285 |
| 2 Adults with 3 children | 91,877 | 77,466 | 133,604 | 45,567 | 24,663 | 90,041 | 209,485 |
| 2 Adults with 4+ children | 48,727 | 60,614 | 198,800 | 46,543 | 43,921 | 70,037 | 287,935 |
| 3+ Adults with 1-2 children | 148,954 | 76,009 | 76,185 | 46,398 | 23,340 | 74,550 | 173,541 |
| 3+ Adults with 3+ children | 141,641 | 83,475 | 155,658 | 36,509 | 59,963 | 86,950 | 333,952 |
| Permanent employee | 151,464 | 73,128 | 65,725 | 42,989 | 17,300 | 89,818 | 128,019 |
| Temporary employee | 141,369 | 55,363 | 65,238 | 30,525 | 30,213 | 50,203 | 116,467 |
| Self employed | 147,036 | 67,379 | 64,731 | 34,190 | 17,618 | 107,136 | 123,224 |
| Sole proprietor | 87,712 | 61,447 | 78,301 | 68,426 | 36,777 | 51,438 | 115,196 |
| Unemployed | 114,801 | 95,532 | 76,659 | 43,169 | 30,602 | 77,566 | 201,139 |
| Pensioner | 197,412 | 80,453 | 69,738 | 38,450 | 14,255 | 90,954 | 208,597 |
| Child care receiver | 123,848 | 98,997 | 84,437 | 38,680 | 16,355 | 59,666 | 197,858 |
| Other | 112,728 | 93,578 | 65,379 | 48,421 | 45,654 | 65,656 | 149,309 |
| All | 179,928 | 79,775 | 66,962 | 42,289 | 18,207 | 86,112 | 162,238 |

Note: These data refer to household level and not to per equivalent adult.

**Table A3.7: Average Amount of Social Transfers (HUF/year) per Household (recipient and non-recipient)**

| | Pension | Unemployment benefit | Family allowance | Child care allowance | Social assistance | Child care fee | All social transfers |
|---|---|---|---|---|---|---|---|
| Below min.pension | 81,365 | 22,286 | 32,949 | 5,357 | 10,339 | 3,221 | 155,517 |
| Btwn min. pension and 2/3 of mean hhold exp. | 104,536 | 16,742 | 27,137 | 3,205 | 5,411 | 2,416 | 159,448 |
| Btwn 2/3 of mean hhold exp. and subsistence min. | 102,500 | 12,905 | 29,318 | 3,168 | 4,141 | 3,589 | 155,620 |
| Above subsistence min. | 82,958 | 10,084 | 30,910 | 2,688 | 3,061 | 5,204 | 134,905 |
| Budapest | 103,267 | 8,175 | 23,535 | 2,504 | 4,275 | 3,782 | 145,538 |
| Towns | 89,057 | 12,016 | 31,697 | 2,738 | 4,274 | 3,915 | 143,697 |
| Villages | 94,101 | 16,696 | 30,946 | 3,756 | 4,106 | 4,207 | 153,812 |
| 1 Male adult | 77,929 | 7,501 | - | - | 1,512 | - | 87,039 |
| 1 Female adult | 111,645 | 1,120 | - | - | 1,700 | - | 114,466 |
| 1 Adult with children | 12,879 | 8,107 | 64,111 | 4,682 | 10,544 | 2,059 | 102,362 |
| 2+ Adults | 144,232 | 12,617 | 9,152 | 74 | 3,089 | 969 | 170,135 |
| 2 Adults with 1-2 children | 10,896 | 18,960 | 58,403 | 9,006 | 4,031 | 11,444 | 112,740 |
| 2 Adults with 3 children | 7,985 | 14,919 | 133,604 | 17,894 | 12,934 | 22,149 | 209,485 |
| 2 Adults with 4+ children | 3,649 | 19,068 | 198,800 | 21,733 | 29,914 | 14,772 | 287,935 |
| 3+ Adults with 1-2 children | 58,687 | 20,478 | 75,757 | 5,106 | 7,864 | 5,274 | 173,166 |
| 3+ Adults with 3+ children | 74,969 | 32,893 | 155,658 | 12,995 | 44,345 | 13,091 | 333,952 |
| Permanent employee | 41,334 | 12,266 | 42,096 | 4,114 | 3,944 | 5,652 | 109,406 |
| Temporary employee | 38,922 | 13,512 | 40,069 | 981 | 15,284 | 2,971 | 111,740 |
| Self employed | 35,520 | 10,238 | 45,511 | 4,170 | 3,068 | 5,571 | 104,078 |
| Sole proprietor | 19,999 | 5,072 | 51,223 | 5,430 | 9,535 | 3,031 | 94,291 |
| Unemployed | 30,352 | 86,268 | 50,965 | 7,870 | 11,734 | 9,324 | 196,514 |
| Pensioner | 197,197 | 4,009 | 3,985 | 219 | 2,973 | 175 | 208,558 |
| Child care receiver | 29,334 | 27,980 | 84,437 | 24,364 | 7,787 | 23,956 | 197,858 |
| Other | 50,707 | 30,542 | 27,132 | 4,118 | 13,026 | 4,056 | 129,581 |
| All | 93,986 | 12,926 | 29,662 | 3,065 | 4,212 | 3,995 | 147,847 |

**Table A3.8: Social Transfers as a Percentage of Household Expenditure and Disposable Income (all households)**

| | Percent of expenditure | | | | | | | | Percent of disposable income |
|---|---|---|---|---|---|---|---|---|---|
| | Pension | Unemployment benefit | Family allowance | Child care allowance | Social assistance | Child care fee | All minus pensions | All social transfers | All social transfers |
| Below min. pension | 76.6 | 13.3 | 16.2 | 3.0 | 6.7 | 1.6 | 40.8 | 117.4 | 66.2 |
| Btwn min. pension and 2/3 of mean hhold exp. | 64.2 | 6.8 | 9.1 | 1.1 | 2.3 | 0.8 | 20.2 | 84.4 | 56.3 |
| Between 2/3 of mean hhold exp. and subsistence min. | 43.3 | 3.8 | 7.2 | 0.8 | 1.3 | 0.9 | 14.1 | 57.4 | 44.2 |
| Above subsistence min. | 21.1 | 2.0 | 4.9 | 0.4 | 0.6 | 0.7 | 8.6 | 29.7 | 27.5 |
| Budapest | 43.2 | 2.8 | 5.0 | 0.6 | 1.2 | 0.5 | 10.1 | 53.3 | 36.4 |
| Towns | 37.4 | 3.7 | 7.5 | 0.7 | 1.5 | 0.8 | 14.3 | 51.7 | 36.4 |
| Villages | 40.8 | 5.3 | 7.6 | 1.0 | 1.5 | 1.0 | 16.4 | 57.2 | 40.6 |
| 1 Male adult | 52.4 | 5.5 | - | - | 1.3 | - | 6.9 | 59.3 | 47.0 |
| 1 Female adult | 83.3 | 0.8 | - | - | 1.4 | - | 2.2 | 85.5 | 72.3 |
| 1 Adult with children | 3.2 | 8.2 | 22.9 | 2.4 | 5.0 | 0.8 | 34.3 | 41.5 | 34.9 |
| 2+ Adults | 51.9 | 4.1 | 2.3 | 0.0 | 1.1 | 0.1 | 7.5 | 59.4 | 42.1 |
| 2 Adults with 1-2 children | 3.0 | 5.7 | 14.1 | 2.5 | 1.1 | 2.6 | 26.0 | 29.0 | 24.2 |
| 2 Adults with 3 children | 1.7 | 4.5 | 29.9 | 4.0 | 3.2 | 3.9 | 45.5 | 47.3 | 39.4 |
| 2 Adults with 4 + children | 1.1 | 4.6 | 48.1 | 5.3 | 7.0 | 3.5 | 68.5 | 69.6 | 58.9 |
| 3 + Adults with 1-2 children | 12.1 | 5.2 | 15.1 | 1.1 | 1.6 | 1.0 | 24.1 | 36.1 | 30.3 |
| 3 + Adults with 3 + children | 17.1 | 7.6 | 35.9 | 2.9 | 11.6 | 3.2 | 61.2 | 78.3 | 60.0 |
| Permanent employee | 10.5 | 3.2 | 9.3 | 1.0 | 1.0 | 1.0 | 15.5 | 26.1 | 22.2 |
| Temporary employee | 16.7 | 4.8 | 14.5 | 0.2 | 7.3 | 0.7 | 27.6 | 44.3 | 37.4 |
| Self employed | 8.6 | 2.4 | 8.7 | 1.2 | 0.7 | 0.9 | 13.9 | 22.6 | 23.3 |
| Sole proprietor | 3.5 | 1.2 | 8.1 | 1.1 | 1.7 | 0.7 | 12.7 | 16.2 | 16.7 |
| Unemployed | 10.9 | 33.4 | 16.3 | 2.6 | 4.9 | 3.2 | 60.4 | 71.2 | 70.1 |
| Pensioner | 95.9 | 1.5 | 1.3 | 0.1 | 1.4 | 0.0 | 4.3 | 100.2 | 86.8 |
| Child care receiver | 5.8 | 9.0 | 28.8 | 10.2 | 3.3 | 8.0 | 59.3 | 65.1 | 59.8 |
| Other | 22.4 | 12.2 | 7.2 | 0.9 | 6.7 | 1.0 | 28.1 | 50.5 | 40.3 |
| All | 39.9 | 4.1 | 7.0 | 0.8 | 1.4 | 0.8 | 14.2 | 54.1 | 37.9 |

| Table A3.9: Poverty Impact of Selected Reforms of the Family Allowance | | | | | | | |
|---|---|---|---|---|---|---|---|
| A. Poverty line = minimum pension (6,400 HUF/mo) | | | | | | | |
| | Actual poverty incidence (%) | Family allowance proposals | | | | | Percentage of households under new benchmark |
| | | FA1 (difference) | FA2 (difference) | FA3 (difference) | FA4 (difference) | FA5 (difference) | |
| 1 Male adult | 4.8 | - | - | - | - | - | 56 |
| 1 Female adult | 5.3 | - | - | - | - | - | 81 |
| 1 Adult with 1 child | 9.2 | - | -3.0 | - | -1.5 | -4.5 | 85 |
| 2+ Adults | 3.3 | - | - | - | - | - | 68 |
| 2 Adults with 1-2 children | 2.8 | +0.1 | +0.1 | - | - | -0.1 | 79 |
| 2 Adults with 3 children | 6.4 | - | -6.4 | - | -0.6 | -6.4 | 94 |
| 2 Adults with 4+ children | 19.0 | - | -19.0 | - | -5.5 | -19.0 | 100 |
| 3+ Adults with 1-2 children | 6.5 | +0.7 | +0.7 | -0.5 | +0.1 | -0.8 | 85 |
| 3+ Adults with 3+ children | 21.4 | - | -18.1 | -7.8 | -6.7 | -18.1 | 100 |
| Permanent employee | 2.6 | +0.2 | -0.3 | -0.1 | +0.1 | -0.4 | 62 |
| Temporary employee | 19.3 | +2.8 | -0.7 | +2.8 | -2.6 | -2.6 | 94 |
| Self-employed | 2.0 | +0.7 | +0.2 | +0.7 | +0.4 | - | 77 |
| Sole proprietor | 2.0 | - | - | - | - | - | 65 |
| Unemployed | 17.5 | - | -4.6 | -2.0 | -2.8 | -6.9 | 95 |
| Pensioner | 5.7 | - | -0.3 | - | - | -0.3 | 90 |
| Child care receiver | 23.6 | - | -13.6 | -3.6 | - | -17.2 | 100 |
| Other | 9.5 | - | -2.7 | -2.7 | -4.8 | -4.8 | 86 |
| Less than primary | 13.1 | - | -1.9 | -1.4 | -3.6 | -3.6 | 95 |
| Primary | 7.3 | +0.4 | -0.5 | -0.1 | +0.4 | -1.0 | 84 |
| Sec. vocational | 2.9 | +0.2 | -0.9 | +0.1 | +0.2 | -1.1 | 76 |
| Special post-primary | 9.8 | - | - | - | - | - | 79 |
| Secondary grammar | 1.3 | - | - | - | - | - | 67 |
| Other secondary | 1.2 | - | - | - | - | - | 60 |
| College | 0.3 | - | -0.2 | - | - | -0.2 | 46 |
| University | 0.0 | - | - | - | - | - | 34 |
| All | 4.5 | +0.1 | -0.7 | -0.2 | -0.2 | -1.0 | 74 |

| | Actual poverty incidence (%) | Family allowance proposals | | | | | Percentage of households under new benchmark |
|---|---|---|---|---|---|---|---|
| | | FA1 (difference) | FA2 (difference) | FA3 (difference) | FA4 (difference) | FA5 (difference) | |
| **Table A3.9: Poverty Impact of Selected Reforms of the Family Allowance (cont'd)** | | | | | | | |
| **B. Poverty line = 2/3 of mean expenditure (10,129 HUF/mo)** | | | | | | | |
| 1 Male adult | 22.6 | - | - | - | - | - | 56 |
| 1 Female adult | 34.7 | - | - | - | - | - | 81 |
| 1 Adult with 1 child | 24.9 | +0.7 | -4.9 | +0.7 | -4.1 | -7.1 | 85 |
| 2+Adults | 22.5 | +0.4 | +0.4 | +0.4 | +0.4 | +0.4 | 68 |
| 2 Adults with 1-2 children | 20.4 | +0.4 | +0.4 | +0.1 | +0.2 | -0.1 | 79 |
| 2 Adults with 3 children | 29.8 | - | -21.5 | -1.4 | -3.2 | -21.5 | 94 |
| 2 Adults with 4+ children | 71.4 | - | -57.3 | -2.5 | - | -57.3 | 100 |
| 3+Adults with 1-2 children | 29.4 | +3.3 | +3.3 | +2.0 | +2.9 | +1.7 | 85 |
| 3+Adults with 3+ children | 72.7 | - | -31.7 | -6.3 | -1.5 | -31.7 | 100 |
| Permanent employee | 18.7 | +1.0 | -0.6 | +0.9 | +0.9 | -0.7 | 62 |
| Temporary employee | 51.3 | - | -3.0 | - | -2.1 | -5.1 | 94 |
| Self-employed | 22.6 | +0.7 | -1.3 | +0.7 | +0.7 | -1.3 | 77 |
| Sole proprietor | 4.7 | +8.7 | +6.0 | +8.7 | +8.7 | +6.0 | 65 |
| Unemployed | 57.4 | - | -11.7 | -7.2 | -1.2 | -15.8 | 95 |
| Pensioner | 35.7 | - | -0.3 | -0.1 | -0.7 | -0.8 | 90 |
| Child care receiver | 54.8 | - | -19.8 | -2.6 | - | -22.3 | 100 |
| Other | 35.6 | +2.1 | -1.8 | +2.1 | -2.3 | -2.3 | 86 |
| Less than primary | 51.0 | - | -1.9 | -0.6 | -3.8 | -3.8 | 95 |
| Primary | 37.3 | +1.0 | -3.1 | +0.3 | +1.0 | -3.4 | 84 |
| Sec. Vocational | 22.7 | +0.9 | -0.9 | +0.7 | +0.9 | -1.2 | 76 |
| Special post-primary | 30.4 | - | - | - | - | - | 79 |
| Secondary grammar | 15.1 | +1.7 | -0.9 | +0.9 | +1.7 | -1.1 | 67 |
| Other secondary | 12.3 | +0.6 | - | +0.1 | +0.6 | -1.1 | 60 |
| College | 5.5 | +0.3 | +0.3 | +0.3 | +0.3 | +0.3 | 46 |
| University | 5.1 | +0.3 | +0.3 | +0.3 | +0.3 | +0.3 | 34 |
| All | 25.3 | +0.8 | -1.3 | +0.3 | +0.4 | -1.7 | 74 |

Note: The family allowance reform proposals are as follows:

FA1 (government proposal): means-testing the family allowance at 25,000 HUF gross income per capita per month (in 1995 HUF and before receipt of the allowance) and instituting an age limit of six years in families of two wage earners and one child.

FA2: FA1 plus additional 3,750 HUF/mo per child in households with 3 or more children.

FA3: FA1 plus additional 3,750 HUF/mo per child in households with 2 or more unemployed members.

FA4: FA1 plus additional 3,750 HUF/mo per child in households where head has less than primary education.

FA5: FA1 plus additional 3,750 HUF/mo per child if either children, unemployment, or education criterion in, respectively, FA2, FA3, or FA4 is met.

**Table A3.10: Poverty Impact of Selected Reforms of Child Care Allowance and Fee, and Social Assistance**

| | A. Poverty line = minimum pension (6,400 HUF/mo) | | | B. Poverty line = 2/3 of mean expenditure (10, 129 HUF/mo) | | |
|---|---|---|---|---|---|---|
| | Actual poverty incidence (%) | Proposal child care allowance and fee (difference) | Proposal social assistance (difference) | Actual poverty incidence (%) | Proposal child care allowance and fee (difference) | Proposal social assistance (difference) |
| 1 Male adult | 4.8 | - | -0.2 | 22.6 | - | -0.2 |
| 1 Female adult | 5.3 | - | -0.5 | 34.7 | - | -0.5 |
| 1 Adult with 1 child | 9.2 | - | -4.8 | 24.9 | +1.4 | -1.1 |
| 2+ Adults | 3.3 | - | -0.6 | 22.5 | +0.1 | -0.5 |
| 2 Adults with 1-2 children | 2.8 | +1.0 | -0.4 | 20.4 | +3.1 | -0.3 |
| 2 Adults with 3 children | 6.4 | +1.9 | -2.0 | 29.8 | +4.4 | -3.6 |
| 2 Adults with 4+ children | 19.0 | +8.2 | -2.6 | 71.4 | +6.8 | -5.6 |
| 3+ Adults with 1-2 children | 6.5 | +0.2 | -1.0 | 29.4 | +1.2 | -0.7 |
| 3+ Adults with 3+ children | 21.4 | +18.5 | -11.4 | 72.7 | +2.4 | - |
| Permanent employee | 2.6 | +0.4 | -0.6 | 18.7 | +1.8 | -0.5 |
| Temporary employee | 19.3 | - | -2.5 | 51.3 | -0.5 | - |
| Self-employed | 2.0 | +1.3 | -0.5 | 22.6 | +0.1 | -0.4 |
| Sole proprietor | 2.0 | - | - | 4.7 | +1.0 | - |
| Unemployed | 17.5 | +4.2 | -3.2 | 57.4 | +2.0 | -2.5 |
| Pensioner | 5.7 | +1.8 | -0.8 | 35.7 | +0.2 | -0.6 |
| Child care receiver | 23.6 | +5.2 | -7.5 | 54.8 | -0.2 | - |
| Other | 9.5 | -2.2 | -0.6 | 35.6 | +1.6 | -1.9 |
| Less than primary | 13.1 | -0.2 | -2.3 | 51.0 | +1.0 | -1.0 |
| Primary | 7.3 | +1.4 | -1.2 | 37.3 | +1.0 | -1.0 |
| Sec. Vocational | 2.9 | +0.7 | -1.0 | 22.7 | +2.0 | -0.6 |
| Special post-primary | 9.8 | - | - | 30.4 | +2.5 | - |
| Secondary grammar | 1.3 | +0.8 | -0.2 | 15.1 | +1.1 | -0.6 |
| Other secondary | 1.2 | +0.8 | - | 12.3 | +1.2 | -0.2 |
| College | 0.3 | -0.3 | -0.3 | 5.5 | +2.0 | -0.4 |
| University | 0.0 | - | - | 5.1 | - | - |
| All | 4.5 | +0.7 | -0.9 | 25.3 | +1.3 | -0.6 |

*Note*: Proposal child care allowance and fee: child care allowance and fee are abolished; child care fee is replaced by a payment of 6,400 HUF/mo (=minimum pension) up to the child's third birthday, if recipient household has income less than 25,000 HUF/mo per capita (prior to the receipt of the family allowance). Proposal social assistance: social assistance is eliminated for households with income over 25,000 HUF/mo per capita (prior to the receipt of the family allowance), and the saved funds are reallocated to the poor in proportion to existing social assistance payments.

| Table A3.11: Ex-ante Targeting of Social Transfers (recipient households) | | | | | |
|---|---|---|---|---|---|
| | Below minimum pension | Between minimum pension and 2/3 of mean household expenditure | Between 2/3 of mean household expenditure and subsistence minimum | Above subsistence minimum | All |
| Pension | 66.9% | 14.6% | 10.2% | 8.2% | 100.0% |
| Unemployment benefit | 26.6% | 30.2% | 23.2% | 20.0% | 100.0% |
| Family allowance | 12.8% | 25.6% | 29.5% | 32.2% | 100.0% |
| Child care allowance | 13.2% | 26.7% | 29.6% | 30.6% | 100.0% |
| Social assistance | 11.0% | 26.4% | 32.3% | 30.3% | 100.0% |
| Child care fee | 11.5% | 25.4% | 33.7% | 29.4% | 100.0% |
| All social transfers | 50.7% | 17.1% | 15.3% | 17.0% | 100.0% |

| Table A3.12: Ex-ante Targeting of Social Transfers (amounts of money) | | | | | |
|---|---|---|---|---|---|
| | Below minimum pension | Between minimum pension and 2/3 of mean household expenditure | Between 2/3 of mean household expenditure and subsistence minimum | Above subsistence minimum | All |
| Pension | 73.6% | 12.1% | 7.8% | 6.5% | 100.0% |
| Unemployment benefit | 36.5% | 27.5% | 20.0% | 16.0% | 100.0% |
| Family allowance | 18.4% | 25.8% | 28.5% | 27.3% | 100.0% |
| Child care allowance | 14.7% | 29.0% | 27.9% | 28.5% | 100.0% |
| Social assistance | 25.1% | 29.1% | 22.3% | 23.5% | 100.0% |
| Child care fee | 13.0% | 21.6% | 27.7% | 37.7% | 100.0% |
| All social transfers | 64.2% | 14.5% | 10.6% | 10.6% | 100.0% |

# Distributors of World Bank Publications

*Prices and credit terms vary from country to country. Consult your local distributor before placing an order.*

**ALBANIA**
Adrion Ltd.
Perlat Rexhepi Str.
Pall. 9, Shk. 1, Ap. 4
Tirana
Tel: (42) 274 19; 221 72
Fax: (42) 274 19

**ARGENTINA**
Oficina del Libro Internacional
Av. Cordoba 1877
1120 Buenos Aires
Tel: (1) 815-8156
Fax: (1) 815-8354

**AUSTRALIA, FIJI, PAPUA NEW GUINEA, SOLOMON ISLANDS, VANUATU, AND WESTERN SAMOA**
D.A. Information Services
648 Whitehorse Road
Mitcham 3132
Victoria
Tel: (61) 3 9210 7777
Fax: (61) 3 9210 7788
URL: http://www.dadirect.com.au

**AUSTRIA**
Gerold and Co.
Graben 31
A-1011 Wien
Tel: (1) 533-50-14-0
Fax: (1) 512-47-31-29

**BANGLADESH**
Micro Industries Development
Assistance Society (MIDAS)
House 5, Road 16
Dhanmondi R/Area
Dhaka 1209
Tel: (2) 326427
Fax: (2) 811188

**BELGIUM**
Jean De Lannoy
Av. du Roi 202
1060 Brussels
Tel: (11) 259-5644
Fax: (11) 258-6990

**BRAZIL**
Publicaçoes Tecnicas Internacionais Ltda.
Rua Peixoto Gomide, 209
01409 Sao Paulo, SP.
Tel: (11) 259-6644
Fax: (11) 258-6990

**CANADA**
Renouf Publishing Co. Ltd.
1294 Algoma Road
Ottawa, Ontario K1B 3W8
Tel: 613-741-4333
Fax: 613-741-5439

**CHINA**
China Financial & Economic
Publishing House
8, Da Fo Si Dong Jie
Beijing
Tel: (1) 333-8257
Fax: (1) 401-7365

**COLOMBIA**
Infoenlace Ltda.
Apartado Aereo 34270
Bogotá D.E.
Tel: (1) 285-2798
Fax: (1) 285-2798

**COTE D'IVOIRE**
Centre d'Edition et de Diffusion
Africaines (CEDA)
04 B.P. 541
Abidjan 04 Plateau
Tel: 225-24-6510
Fax: 225-25-0567

**CYPRUS**
Center of Applied Research
Cyprus College
6, Diogenes Street, Engomi
P.O. Box 2006
Nicosia
Tel: 244-1730
Fax: 246-2051

**CZECH REPUBLIC**
National Information Center
prodejna, Konviktska 5
CS – 113 57 Prague 1
Tel: (2) 2422-9433
Fax: (2) 2422-1484
URL: http://www.nis.cz/

**DENMARK**
SamfundsLitteratur
Rosenoerns Allé 11
DK-1970 Frederiksberg C
Tel: (31)-351942
Fax: (31)-357822

**ECUADOR**
Facultad Latinoamericana de
Ciencias Sociales
FLASCO-SEDE Ecuador
Calle Ulpiano Paez 118
y Av. Patria
Quito, Ecuador
Tel: (2) 542 714; 542 716; 528 200
Fax: (2) 566 139

**EGYPT, ARAB REPUBLIC OF**
Al Ahram
Al Galaa Street
Cairo
Tel: (2) 578-6083
Fax: (2) 578-6833

The Middle East Observer
41, Sherif Street
Cairo
Tel: (2) 393-9732
Fax: (2) 393-9732

**FINLAND**
Akateeminen Kirjakauppa
Oltig an ISoIkhhar
FIN-00371 Helsinki
Tel: (0) 12141
Fax: (0) 121-4441
URL: http://booknet.cultnet.fi/aka/

**FRANCE**
World Bank Publications
66, avenue d'Iéna
75116 Paris
Tel: (1) 40-69-30 55
Fax: (1) 40-69-30 68

**GERMANY**
UNO-Verlag
Poppelsdorfer Allee 55
53115 Bonn
Tel: (228) 212940
Fax: (228) 217492

**GREECE**
Papasotiriou S.A.
35, Stournara Str.
106 82 Athens
Tel: (1) 364-1826
Fax: (1) 364-8254

**HONG KONG, MACAO**
Asia 2000 Ltd.
Sales & Circulation Department
Seabird House, unit 1101-02
22-28 Wyndham Street, Central
Hong Kong
Tel: 852 2530-1409
Fax: 852 2526-1107
URL: http://www.sales@asia2000.com.hk

**HUNGARY**
Foundation for Market
Economy
Dombovari UI 17-19
H-1117 Budapest
Tel: 36 1 204 2951 or
36 1 204 2948
Fax: 36 1 204 2953

**INDIA**
Allied Publishers Ltd.
751 Mount Road
Madras – 600 002
Tel: (44) 852-3938
Fax: (44) 852-0649

**INDONESIA**
Pt. Indira Limited
Jalan Borobudur 20
P.O. Box 181
Jakarta 10320
Tel: (21) 390-4290
Fax: (21) 421-4289

**IRAN**
Kowkab Publishers
P.O. Box 19575-511
Tehran
Tel: (21) 258-3723
Fax: 98 (21) 258-3723

Ketab Sara Co. Publishers
Khaled Estamboli Ave.,
6th Street
Kusheh Delafrooz No. 8
Tehran
Tel: 8717819 or 8716104
Fax: 8862479

**IRELAND**
Government Supplies Agency
Oifig an tSolathair
4-5 Harcourt Road
Dublin 2
Tel: (1) 461-3111
Fax: (1) 475-2670

**ISRAEL**
Yozmot Literature Ltd.
P.O. Box 56055
Tel Aviv 61560
Tel: (3) 5285-397
Fax: (3) 5285-397

R.O.Y. International
PO Box 13056
Tel Aviv 61130
Tel: (3) 5461423
Fax: (3) 5461442

Palestinian Authority/Middle East
Index Information Services
P.O.B. 19502 Jerusalem
Tel: (22) 271219

**ITALY**
Licosa Commissionaria Sansoni SPA
Via Duca Di Calabria, 1/1
Casella Postale 552
50125 Firenze
Tel: (55) 645-415
Fax: (55) 641-257

**JAMAICA**
Ian Randle Publishers Ltd.
206 Old Hope Road
Kingston 6
Tel: 809-927-2085
Fax: 809-977-0243

**JAPAN**
Eastern Book Service
Hongo 3-Chome,
Bunkyo-ku 113
Tokyo
Tel: (03) 3818-0861
Fax: (03) 3818-0864
URL: http://www.bekkoame or jp/~svt-ebs

**KENYA**
Africa Book Service (E.A.) Ltd.
Quaran House, Mfangano Street
P.O. Box 45245
Nairobi
Tel: (2) 23641
Fax: (2) 330272

**KOREA, REPUBLIC OF**
Daejon Trading Co. Ltd.
P.O. Box 34
Yeoeida
Seoul
Tel: (2) 785-1631/4
Fax: (2) 784-0315

**MALAYSIA**
University of Malaya Cooperative
Bookshop, Limited
P.O. Box 1127
Jalan Pantai Baru
59700 Kuala Lumpur
Tel: (3) 756-5000
Fax: (3) 755-4424

**MEXICO**
INFOTEC
Apartado Postal 22-860
14060 Tlalpan.
Mexico D.F.
Tel: (5) 606-0011
Fax: (5) 606-0386

**NETHERLANDS**
De Lindeboom/InOr-Publikaties
P.O. Box 202
7480 AE Haaksbergen

**NEW ZEALAND**
EBSCO NZ Ltd.
Private Mail Bag 99914
New Market
Auckland
Tel: (9) 524-8119
Fax: (9) 524-8067

**NIGERIA**
University Press Limited
Three Crowns Building Jericho
Private Mail Bag 5095
Ibadan
Tel: (22) 41-1356
Fax: (22) 41-2056

**NORWAY**
Narvesen Information Center
Book Department
P.O. Box 6125 Etterstad
N-0602 Oslo 6
Tel: (22) 57-3300
Fax: (22) 68-1901

**PAKISTAN**
Mirza Book Agency
65, Shahrah-e-Quaid-e-Azam
Lahore 54000
Tel: (42) 7353601
Fax: (42) 7585283

Oxford University Press
5 Bangalore Town
Sharae Faisal
PO Box 13033
Karachi-75350
Tel: (21) 446307
Fax: (21) 454-7640

**PERU**
Editorial Desarrollo SA
Apartado 3824
Lima 1
Tel: (14) 285380
Fax: (14) 286628

**PHILIPPINES**
International Booksource Center Inc.
Suite 720, Cityland 10
Condominium Tower 2
H.V dela Costa, corner
Valero St.
Makati, Metro Manila
Tel: (2) 817-9676
Fax: (2) 817-1741

**POLAND**
International Publishing Service
UI. Piekna 31/37
00-577 Warzawa
Tel: (2) 628-6089
Fax: (2) 621-7255

**PORTUGAL**
Livraria Portugal
Rua Do Carmo 70-74
1200 Lisbon
Tel: (1) 347-4982
Fax: (1) 347-0264

**ROMANIA**
Compani De Librarii Bucuresti S.A.
Str. Lipscani no. 26, sector 3
Bucharest
Tel: (1) 613 9645
Fax: (1) 312 4000

**RUSSIAN FEDERATION**
Isdatelstvo <Ves Mir>
9a, Lolpachnul pereulok
Moscow 101831
Tel: (95) 917 87 49
Fax: (95) 917 92 59

**SAUDI ARABIA, QATAR**
Jarir Book Store
P.O. Box 3196
Riyadh 11471
Tel: (1) 477-3140
Fax: (1) 477-2940

**SINGAPORE, TAIWAN,
MYANMAR, BRUNEI**
Asahgate Publishing Asia
Pacific Pte. Ltd.
41 Kallang Pudding Road #04-03
Golden Wheel Building
Singapore 349316
Tel: (65) 741-5166
Fax: (65) 742-9356

**SLOVAK REPUBLIC**
Slovart G.T.G. Ltd.
Krupinska 4
PO Box 152
852 99 Bratislava 5
Tel: (7) 839472
Fax: (7) 839485

**SOUTH AFRICA, BOTSWANA**
For single titles:
Oxford University Press
Southern Africa
P.O. Box 1141
Cape Town 8000
Tel: (21) 45-7266
Fax: (21) 45-7265

For subscription orders:
International Subscription Service
P.O. Box 41095
Craighall
Johannesburg 2024
Tel: (11) 880-1448
Fax: (11) 880-6248

**SPAIN**
Mundi-Prensa Libros. S.A.
Castello 37
28001 Madrid
Tel: (1) 431-3399
Fax: (1) 575-3998
http://www.tsai.es/mprensa

Libreria Internacional AEDOS
Consell de Cent. 391
08009 Barcelona
Tel: (3) 488-3009
Fax: (3) 487-7659

**SRI LANKA, THE MALDIVES**
Lake House Bookshop
P.O. Box 244
100, Sir Chittampalam A.
Gardiner Mawatha
Colombo 2
Tel: (1) 32105
Fax: (1) 432104

**SWEDEN**
Fritzes Customer Service
Regeringsgaton 12
S-106 47 Stockholm
Tel: (8) 690 90 90
Fax: (8) 21 47 77

Wennergren-Williams AB
P. O. Box 1305
S-171 25 Solna
Tel: (8) 705-97-50
Fax: (8) 27-00-71

**SWITZERLAND**
Librairie Payot
Service Institutionnel
Côtes-de-Montbenon 30
1002 Lausanne
Tel: (021)-320-2511
Fax: (021)-320-2514

Van Diermen Editions Technique
Ch. de Lacuez 41
CH1807 Blonay
Tel: (021) 943 2673
Fax: (021) 943 3605

**TANZANIA**
Oxford University Press
Maktaba Street
PO Box 5299
Dar es Salaam
Tel: (51) 29209
Fax: (51) 46822

**THAILAND**
Central Books Distribution
306 Silom Road
Bangkok
Tel: (2) 235-5400
Fax: (2) 237-8321

**TRINIDAD & TOBAGO, JAMAICA**
Systematics Studies Unit
#9 Watts Street
Curepe
Trinidad, West Indies
Tel: 809-662-5654
Fax: 809-662-5654

**UGANDA**
Gustro Ltd.
Madhvani Building
PO Box 9997
Plot 16/4 Jinja Rd.
Kampala
Tel/Fax: (41) 254763

**UNITED KINGDOM**
Microinfo Ltd.
P.O. Box 3
Alton, Hampshire GU34 2PG
England
Tel: (1420) 86848
Fax: (1420) 89889

**ZAMBIA**
University Bookshop
Great East Road Campus
P.O. Box 32379
Lusaka

**ZIMBABWE**
Longman Zimbabwe (Pte.) Ltd.
Tourle Road, Ardbennie
P.O. Box ST125
Southerton
Harare
Tel: (4) 662711
Fax: (4) 662716